PLAYING THE OFFENSIVE LINE

A COMPREHENSIVE GUIDE
for COACHES and PLAYERS

Karl Nelson & Bob O'Connor

McGraw·Hill

New York   Chicago   San Francisco   Lisbon   London   Madrid   Mexico City
Milan   New Delhi   San Juan   Seoul   Singapore   Sydney   Toronto

Library of Congress Cataloging-in-Publication Data

Nelson, Karl, 1960–
    Playing the offensive line : a comprehensive guide for coaches and players /
Karl Nelson & Bob O'Connor.
        p.   cm.
    Includes index.
    ISBN 0-07-145149-8 (alk. paper)
    1. Football—Offense.   2. Football—Coaching.   I. O'Connor, Robert,
1932–   II. Title.

    GV951.8.N45   2006
    796.332'07'7—dc22   2005017228

1 2 3 4 5 6 7 8 9 0   DOC/DOC   0 9 8 7 6 5

ISBN 0-07-145149-8

This book is printed on acid-free paper.

Contents

Foreword

I t's about time we had an outstanding book on offensive line play. The offensive line is the key unit for football success. To play effectively on the line you must be intelligent, have knowledge of the fundamentals, and then drill, drill, drill.

Karl and Bob have covered every base in offensive line play. The book gives every coach and offensive lineman a comprehensive look at what may be done to be an effective blocker. From drive, scramble, wedge, zone, and double-team blocking to special requirements for snappers, special teams, and the intricacies of pass protection, this book gives you the whole picture.

But more than techniques, Karl and Bob have given up-to-date information on nutrition, strength training, and the mental requirements for successful line play. Herein, you will find it all.

Karl, of course, is an expert on how to play offensive line. First as an All-American at Iowa State, then as a stalwart right tackle for the Giants, including our victory in Super Bowl XXI, then as an assistant while he made a courageous recovery from Hodgkin's disease. I was happy to see that he wrote about his successful battle with cancer in the book. Karl was an intelligent player who played from the heart. He came to the Giants as a rookie with raw talent, and by the time he was done, he was a seasoned veteran who had learned how to really play the game. I know working on this book was a labor of love for Karl, and I think he did himself proud in his efforts. I was particularly interested in his reflections on situations and encounters with other players which he interspersed through the book. It made the reading more personal and lively.

Bob is one of the longest-standing members of the American Football Coaches Association. He has coached at every level from junior high through the major university levels and with two Super Bowl coaches, Ray Malavasi and Tom Flores. Now in his "retirement," he is back coaching high school ball as a head coach in California. Bob is the author, with Tom Flores, of the bestselling coaching book *Coaching Football* and has recently completed a book with Al Groh titled *Coaching the Special Situations*. You will enjoy the reading, and it will increase your ability to play or coach the offensive line. I definitely recommend this groundbreaking book.

—Bill Parcells, Head Coach, Dallas Cowboys

Preface

In a recent interview, Joe Gibbs, the Washington Redskins head coach, said that what he looks for first is character. After that it is intelligence. Ability is only third in his priorities. If you don't have character you will not even play football, let alone offensive line. As you may know, the offensive linemen continually score higher in intelligence than any other players in the pro ranks. Quarterbacks rank second. The ability to play in the offensive line is primarily a learned skill. It is a unique ability on the football team—and it is essential. Nearly every high-level coach will tell you that the offensive line is the most important unit on the football team. Without effective blocking you can't run and you can't pass—so it is rather difficult to score.

There is no one way to teach offensive line fundamentals. The stance and the types of blocks you will employ will be determined by your offensive theory. If you are using a very quick-hitting offense you might choose to use a four-point stance and scramble blocking (on all fours). If you are a run-and-shoot passing team you will probably use a balanced three-point stance or even a two-point stance.

In this book we lay out the fundamentals needed to coach or to play in the offensive line. We cover different types of one-on-one blocking, double-teaming, zoning, wedging, pulling, trapping, goal line blocking, and all of the other physical and mental skills you need to coach or play the offensive line.

Of course there is more than the physical side of play. The mental side is at least as important. We talk about the mental aspects of the game and the mental aspects of life. While football often mirrors life with its opportunities for cooperation and competition, its emphasis is on goal setting and working hard to achieve those goals, and the joy of victory and the agony of defeat—there is a bigger life out there. Our families and our jobs will take up a major part of most of our lives. But there is no question that playing football helps to prepare

us for our lives. And playing the offensive line offers more opportunities to prepare for a successful life than any other position on the team—or any other
sport. Be grateful that you are coaching or playing on the most important unit
of the most important game.

Key to Diagrams

C = Center
G = Guard
T = Tackle
E = End
DT = Defensive Tackle
DE = Defensive End
LB = Linebacker

Preparing to Play Safely

layers' equipment is not always properly fitted. Many coaches at the lower levels seem to believe that just putting pads on the shoulders is enough, and that simply handing a boy a helmet will do the job of protecting him from blows to the head. This is not the case.

Helmets

The helmet is the most important piece of football equipment. The suspension or padding inside the hard plastic shell does the job of redirecting the blow around the shell to the skull to reduce the chance of a concussion.

A reputable brand of helmet should be chosen. Riddell has done extensive research on helmet effectiveness and believes that its new Revolution brand is superior to other brands. But Adams, Schutt, and Nakona all make effective helmets as well. After purchase, it is essential to have the helmets recertified yearly by approved football equipment reconditioners. Outside of the United States players seldom or never have their helmets tested for protection. The padding may have hardened, the air sacks may not hold air, the plastic may be cracked. Because of these factors there is an increased number of serious head injuries in those wearing the untested helmets.

Proper helmet fit requires that the helmet not be too loose (a thumb should not fit inside the front of the crown) nor too tight (where the air pressure, jaw pads, or other cushioning pads squeeze on the head, possibly causing headaches).

Air cushions should be inflated until the helmet is comfortable, but does not squeeze the head. The jaw pads should hold the helmet shell comfortably away from the chinbone, leaving an eighth of an inch of air between the chinbone and the pad. The chin strap should securely hold the helmet in place.

Shoulder Pads

Shoulder pads that are too large do not protect the collarbone, while those too small do not protect the shoulder joint. Check that the front of the pad adequately covers the collarbone and that the shoulder cup is free to cover the shoulder joint. The pads should be secured so that they are fairly tight fitting and don't slip around on the shoulders.

Ankles Braces

Ankle injuries are the most common injuries in football—so it is wise to do all in your power to protect yourself. That is why taping for games and practices became so common. But now we have found that tape begins to lose its effectiveness in ten to fifteen minutes, so ankle braces have become the standard method of preventing ankle injuries. In the long run braces are 50 to 60 percent cheaper per year than tape, and they are far more effective. Ankle braces should not only be used when playing and practicing football, but also when playing basketball and other sports in which ankle injuries are possible. When an ankle is sprained the ligaments are stretched. It may take years for them to shrink back to where they were before the sprain. It is therefore wise to prevent that first sprain. This is why most high-level programs minimize taping but require ankle braces.

Ankle braces should be mandatory for practice and games. They can be purchased in most sporting goods stores and on the Internet—where they are usually cheaper. Linemen can use wraparound stiff supports (not elastic ankle supports). These generally cost $15 to $20 each. The higher-end plastic braces that backs are more likely to use cost nearly twice as much. Wraparound cloth lace-up braces are cheaper but limit ankle flexibility. This can reduce the potential speed of the player. Plastic-sided braces allow more running flexibility. Either kind should last for years.

Knee Braces

Heavy metal braces are used by most college and professional linemen. They can protect the knees from blows from the side. Research indicates that braces protect the knees when the player is fresh, but as he tires he can have more knee injuries. The heavy metal fatigues the leg muscles faster than playing without a brace. So if you are planning on using a knee brace, develop very strong legs.

When I was with the Giants, the offensive and defensive linemen were encouraged to wear knee braces that were held on with straps. They were a little bulky and some guys said that they made their legs tired and heavy. Most of the defensive players didn't like to wear them and did only when the coaches threatened to fine them unless they did. They were not required to wear them in the games, and they did not. I always wore them, even in games, and I am glad I did. There were always at least five times during any year that the braces saved my knees. By the end of the year, the piece of metal that protected my knee had been bent in at least half an inch. The way I looked at it was that getting in better shape so my legs were not tired and wearing the braces was better than blowing out my knee, or at least stretching things that should not be stretched. If these braces are available where you coach, I would strongly advise you to get them for your linemen.

Use Proper Fundamentals

Proper fundamentals are a major method of preventing injuries. "Keep the head out of football" is the maxim of the American Football Coaches Association. Death or paralysis can be prevented by using proper equipment and proper technique. If the head is down during a block the vertebrae are placed in a weakened position, and crushed discs, a broken neck, or other serious injuries may occur.

Playing with Injuries

Injuries are a fact of life in football. Football is a collision sport, but if you are properly conditioned, you can absorb the punishment without injury. Younger players, such as Pop Warner players in age groups from ten to twelve, are usually not fast or strong enough to do serious damage to each other. The pads are so big and bulky on them that their movement may be limited. There are actually more injuries in Little League Soccer than there are in Little League Football.

I have been to many football awards dinners over the years, and I have seen some things that disturbed me. Young players should not play through injuries like professional players do. At one dinner a player who was about twelve years old was praised by his coach for playing with a broken jaw. Another time there was a young player who played with a broken arm even though the doctor did not think it was a good idea. No game is worth risking doing permanent damage to a young player. I even question things I have seen in high school and college. When I was a senior in high school I pulled a muscle in my back and I played through it. There were plays that I could barely scrape myself off the field after the play, but I always made it back to the huddle and back to the line for the next play. With backs you never know, but I had very bad back problems in college that cost me at least being drafted one round lower than I should have been. I was young and stupid at the time, but if I knew in high school what I know now, I would have taken a week off and gotten better.

There is a difference between pain and injury, but the coach must err on the side of safety with young players. The pros are paid to play with an injury that, if they play, will not get worse but will cause pain. In a playoff game against the Rams in 1984, I had been tripped and was on my back. A player landed on my stomach, just below my ribs. Then the rest of the pile landed on both of us. The weight pulled two ribs off the cartilage at the base of my ribcage. I came out so they could put a flak jacket on me, and I went back into the game. I even played the next week when we lost to the 49ers. That was one of the most painful things that I ever went through, but I couldn't get hurt worse if I played, so I played.

I did not get a shot to help the pain from my ribcage injury because I wanted to know what was going on. The Giants gave out very few shots to help people play, but there were other teams in the NFL that did, and I think that is wrong. Under no circumstance should a Pop Warner player get a shot to play, and I don't think that high school players should either. I always think of the player in the movie *North Dallas Forty* who took a shot for his hamstring and blew it out in a game because he couldn't feel how bad it was.

Recently a coach got in trouble for giving out a "crybaby award" to a player at an awards dinner. That is just stupid. Football should be seen and used as a teaching tool and learning tool for kids, not as a place for an adult to feel superior over kids by getting in a position of authority. This is the type of guy that gives coaches a bad name. He is the "other" coach in all those movies like *Little Giants* who are egomaniacs and think that their success as a coach is more important than the development of the kids or the educationally positive things that football can teach.

2

Stance and Alignment

S tance and alignment are the first steps in the process of a lineman completing his assignment. A bad stance puts him at a huge disadvantage. Football is a hard enough game without self-imposed limitations.

Stance

The classic offensive lineman stance starts with the feet slightly wider than shoulder width apart but not more than four to six inches wider. Generally the inside of the feet will align with the outside of the shoulders. The spread of the feet may vary depending on the type of offense run or the stature of the player. If the linemen nearly always block straight ahead, as in the old split-T formation, the feet may be narrower. If the linemen pull a great deal they might be slightly wider. A tall, thinner player might have his feet wider and a stockier, squatty player might have his feet closer to shoulder width.

If the player is right-handed, he will drop his right foot back before he goes down. The front of the toes of the right foot should line up with the middle of the left foot. The toes should always point directly forward. This sounds like a minor point, but it is very important. The body will go where the toes point it to go, and if the toes are pointing out, when you push off to get out of your stance, part of the force you will exert will go sideways. This reduces the amount of force or power delivered forward.

Some people, because of lack of flexibility or the way their body is put together, have a problem getting their toes to go forward. Do everything you can to get them as forward as possible. This will help in the long run. Some coaches will teach the stance with the toes slightly inward, since most people toe out, and if they feel that their toes are pointed inward they may actually be straight ahead—where they are supposed to be.

With the feet slightly wider than shoulder width apart, strong foot back, and toes forward, have the player squat down and put his elbows on his knees. This will put him in a good football position. Next have him lean forward to put his hand on the ground. This is the three-point stance. The shoulders should be square to the line of scrimmage and at the same level, not with one shoulder lower than the other. The off arm should have the forearm resting on the knee. The head needs to be up so the player can see in front of him (see photos 2.1 and 2.2). The back should be flat, or possibly even arched a little. The shoulders should be pulled back rather than hunched forward. Younger players tend to hump their backs toward the sky and to hunch their shoulders. If they delivered a blow in this position, it would hurt the back, and the blow delivered would be very soft.

The amount of weight that should be placed on the hand depends on what type of offense you are running. If you run the ball over 90 percent of the time

Photo 2.1 Three-point stance (front)

Photo 2.2 Three-point stance (side)

and most of the blocking schemes you use call for the lineman to go straight forward, then the lineman can have a lot of weight on his hand so his momentum will go forward when he picks up his hand. If this is the case, you may even want to consider having the lineman in a four-point stance (see photos 2.3 and 2.4). To do this, simply have the player drop his off hand, having both hands in line with the line of scrimmage. One foot should still be back a little. The back also needs to stay straight, and the shoulders need to be pulled back.

If you throw the ball some or your players are expected to be able to take side steps or pull, then a three-point stance is necessary. Less weight should be on the hand. Pro coaches want players to be able to pick up their hand from this stance and not fall forward or even move their feet to regain balance. The hand should not be put as far out in front, and more weight should be kept back on the feet. This balanced stance will allow the player to come up and pass protect very quickly and will also easily allow the player to pull in either direction. The off arm should have the forearm resting on the knee.

The thumb and the first three fingers should always be put on the ground. If it feels comfortable the little finger can also be on the ground. I felt more athletic in my stance without having the pinky down. I have seen some people teach putting the fist down instead of the fingers. While this was the standard method in the early years of football, it is seldom used today. It makes the player have

Photo 2.3 Balanced four-point stance

Photo 2.4 Four-point stance with forward lean

too much weight forward and drops the front of the body too low to be able to come out of the stance easily. Also, the fingers give much better balance in the stance. Some people teach having the weight on the second bone of the fingers. This may be more comfortable for some people. But having the fingers down allows for a better push-off when pass blocking or pulling.

Not everyone can use the classic stance. We see many "bad" stances used by very good players. The Minnesota Vikings had a guard, Randall McDaniel, who had the ugliest stance I ever saw. His back foot was out wide, and his toe was pointing almost to the sideline. How he ever got anything done out of this stance I don't know, but since he made a few pro bowls, I guess he did OK. You have to work with any physical limitations a player may have, such as flexibility or a natural in-toeing or out-toeing of the feet. Find what works best for him.

In the pros, you will see that linemen on the right side of the line will have their right hand down, and on the left side they will have their left hand down. This is better for drop back pass protection. On the other hand, many high school and college teams will take an opposite hand position—left hand down on the right side and right hand down on the left side. This makes it easier to pull across the center for traps and power plays.

Since college and high school players are more likely to run the ball and pros more likely to pass it, you can understand the different preferences. Still, it is not easy for a natural righty to get in a left-handed stance, especially a younger player. The disadvantages of an awkward stance probably will outweigh the advantages of having the outside hand down and outside foot back unless the person is extremely coordinated.

Make sure the players are using the same exact stance every play, whether it be a run or a pass. It is a huge disadvantage to let the defense know if the play is going to be a run or a pass because the linemen are tipping it off. Players who pull sometimes alter their stance so they can get out of the stance and in the right direction quickly. This will lead the defense directly to the point of attack, and the play will have very little chance of success. Defenders look for heavy weight on the hands (more light skin in the fingers), indicating a run, or for a darker color in the fingers, indicating less weight on them and signaling a pass. Defenders will also look at the linemen to see if they are leaning—indicating a pulling action.

To get out of the stance and moving forward, the player should throw back the hand on the ground and step first with the back foot. Staying low out of the stance is essential for quickness and also to deliver a blow. To emphasize this, use a bar, approximately six to twelve inches higher than the player's head in his stance. The players should line up about a yard behind the bar and run under it. If they hit their head, they are not coming out low enough. This should be used for practice and should be done at the start of each practice.

The first step out of the stance is extremely important and, if not taken correctly, will not allow success, even if everything else is done properly. For a straight-ahead block, the first step should be taken with the back foot and be made directly forward.

If the play is going to the left from where the lineman is, then the first step needs to be taken with the left foot, stepping out at a 45-degree angle. This will allow him to get to a point outside the man in front of him and hook him, stopping him from getting to the point of attack. If there is a linebacker directly in front, this is even more important because the backer will read the flow of the play and start moving to his right immediately. If the lineman goes straight ahead and then follows the backer, he will run him directly into the play. The lineman needs to go to where the backer will be *after* he reads the play, not to where he starts the play. This sounds logical, but it is a common mistake with younger players.

The same is true for going to the right. The first step must be made with the right foot at a 45-degree angle, even if this is the foot that is forward in the stance. This will be natural for a right-handed person and is essential for success.

A great drill for this is to have the players in their stance and call out "right," "left," or "straight" and then immediately say "go." Have the players take the first step only and see exactly where the first step goes. This will make them have a balanced stance. Make sure they are using the correct stance each time, the one they will be using in a game.

Alignment

Alignment includes both the distance the player will line up from the line of scrimmage and the split he will take from the next lineman in. The type of offense run will be a major factor in how the linemen will align.

The line of scrimmage is the area between the two ends of the ball and stretches from sideline to sideline and from the field to the sky. Only the snapper (the official name for the center) is allowed to penetrate that zone. In some offenses the snapper is urged to get as close as possible to the line of scrimmage. In others he is expected to be as far from the line as possible while still being able to grip the ball and snap it.

If the offense is a quick-hitting attack, the players are generally asked to be as close to the line of scrimmage as possible so they can attack the defense quickly (see photo 2.5). In the slower attacks using a deep-set tailback and/or zone blocking, the linemen are usually asked to be as deep as possible. This means that the guards, tackles, and ends will line their heads at the belt, or sometimes the lower end of the number, of the center (see photo 2.6). Aligning deeper allows the blockers to see the charge of the defenders as the offensive linemen are taking their position step and their power step as they make their blocks. This is particularly important in zone blocking.

The split of the linemen is of critical importance. In a power offense the split may be six inches or less. This allows for more effective double-teams and wedges and reduces the ability of linebackers to stunt into wide gaps. It also allows the offense to get to the end more quickly. Of course if the splits are minimal the blockers must physically move the defenders to make a hole.

Wider splits create horizontal or vertical holes. (The distance of a linebacker from the line of scrimmage creates a vertical hole.) Either type of hole is valuable to the offense in a quick-hitting attack. With a very wide split the blocker merely needs to occupy the defender. Old-timers will remember the split-T attack in which the offensive linemen could take splits of four to six feet—or even more if the defender would stay head up on him.

Today most offenses prefer a split of one to three feet between the linemen. Some teams use two feet between all linemen or a one-foot split between the center and guard and a two-foot split between the guard and tackle. The tight end may then be two or three feet outside the tackle. While it is quite easy to zone block from a two-foot split, the wedge or double-team blocks become more difficult.

As in every phase of football—every formation, play, alignment, or technique—you gain something and you lose something with each variation. Each nuance of the stance, alignment, or split gives you advantages and disadvantages. It is up to the coach to weigh these advantages and disadvantages for each phase of his offense.

Photo 2.5 Alignment close to the line of scrimmage for a quick-hitting attack

Photo 2.6 A deeper alignment for zone blocking or other slower attack: helmets on center's number

┌─────┐
│ 3 │
└─────┘

Drive and Shoulder Blocking

The key to most offenses is being able to run the ball. The run sets up the passing game by making the defense hesitate before they can drop into their coverages. It also keeps the defensive linemen honest by having to play run first rather than just teeing off on the offense and rushing the passer. The running game also sets the tone of the game. There is no quicker way to take control of a game and demoralize an opponent than to run the ball down their throats.

In 1986, the year the Giants won the Super Bowl, we generally had about fifteen running plays in the game plan, but we ran four of those plays about 80 percent of the time. If you can execute the blocking schemes, you should be able to tell the opponent where you are going to run and still have positive plays. We generally ran the ball on first and second down, and then, if we had to, we threw it on third down to get the first.

The Drive Block

The running game starts with the basic drive block where the lineman is in a one-on-one situation with a defender on the line directly across from him. His job is to drive the man off the line of scrimmage and keep him occupied so the back can pick the hole on either side to run through. With so many teams using a deep running back, such as an I-formation, it is imperative that the block be

The best defensive end against the run I ever played against, I also practiced with every day. His name is Curtis McGriff. I am sure that you have not heard about him, because he was not flashy, mouthy, or obnoxious. All he did was stop the run. Don't take my word on this. Jackie Slater, who played for the Rams for twenty years, was asked who the top ten people were that he had to block. At the top of the list was Curtis McGriff. He was listed above another of my teammates, Lawrence Taylor, so you know what Jackie thought of Curtis. Curtis couldn't get off the ball to pass rush, but you rarely moved him off the line of scrimmage. Bill Parcells said he knew that I would make it when, during a goal line drill in training camp of 1984, I moved Curtis back about a foot. He said that he had never seen that before, and my stock went up dramatically.

sustained a long time. The rule change that allowed offensive blockers to use their hands has been largely instrumental in allowing blockers to maintain contact longer and in allowing deeper-set backs to pick and choose whatever openings occur in the defensive line. It has allowed the offense to take advantage of openings created by defensive slants and stunts and has allowed for cutback plays when the defense has pursued too quickly to the flow of the play.

To start the drive block, as always, the lineman needs to be in a good stance. On the snap of the ball, drive the down hand backward while taking a short six- to twelve-inch step with the back foot. The head should stay low, looking up at a target of the top of the numbers, under the shoulder pads. If the hole is right over the blocker, the head should be in the middle. If the hole is to the gap on either side of the blocker, the head should aim for the number to that side. You block with your eyes, so have your eyes on your target—the top of the numbers. Your back must stay flat, parallel to the ground, and slightly arched. The next step is the power step with the other foot. You should try to get this foot to about where the defender had his down hand in his stance. During this step, bring both hands up and into the chest of the defender, lifting him up. This can be done either with closed fists, or preferably, with an open hand to give better control (see photo 3.1). The hands should be as close together as possible and inside those of the defender. The man with his hands closer together usually wins.

Once contact is made, start to lift with the arms. Be sure that your elbows are down and close together because you can't lift effectively if your elbows are out. The feet need to keep driving forward in short, choppy steps, keeping them about six inches wider than shoulder width apart.

Photo 3.1 Approach for the drive block: the hands should be close together, inside the defender's hands

The power and lift of the drive block come from the hips and low back. Once contact is made, the hips should drop by arching the back, allowing the use of the largest muscles in the body—the legs, butt, and low back—to do the work. Have the hips move forward and upward while lifting the defender with the arms (see photo 3.2 on the next page). Keep the feet moving, trying to step on the toes of the defender. If you drive and lift hard enough, you will pancake your opponent by putting him on his back, flat as a pancake. This is best done by exploding the arms upward once you are chest-to-chest and driving. Remember the two laws of blocking: the low man wins, and inside hands win.

I learned the lesson of inside hands while blocking Reggie White. He always tried to get his hands inside mine when I was blocking him, on both the run and the pass. He was controlling me more easily than other defensive ends because of this. It didn't take me long to figure it out, and I focused on getting my hands inside of his and had much more success. I battled him so hard getting my hands inside that I sprained both of my thumbs, having them bent backward. I went home after the game and couldn't even pick up my nine-month-old daughter because of my thumbs, but I did have a good day against Reggie.

The most common mistake young players make is that they try to make the initial hit as hard as they can. They take the first two steps and then stop their feet, almost lunging at the defender. They may hit hard, but against a good player they will fall off or be easily thrown off because of bad balance. They must envision running *through* the defender, not just hitting him. This is the same as a karate instructor telling students to aim for a spot six inches past the board they are trying to break. If they hit only to the board, they will break their hand, not the board.

Photo 3.2 Lifting the opponent in the drive block: the low man wins

A defensive player has to read what is going on behind you. When he pops his head up to take a look, that is when you can exert pressure on him and get some movement. You are never going to drive Reggie five yards off the ball. With him, you want to do more of a controlled block, keeping him occupied so he cannot come off and make the play. If you have a player who is not as strong or as big as the guy he is lining up against, this is a good tactic to take. Here is where technique and determination can overcome strength and size.

Balance is very important to the drive block. If you do not have good balance, it will be easy for the defender to throw you off, no matter how hard you hit him. Keep the feet about six inches wider than shoulder width, taking short, choppy steps, keeping one foot on the ground at all times. Work to have all body parts working together in the same direction: toes, knees, hips, and shoulders should all be directly facing the target. Some younger linemen may try to turn their body while drive blocking, thinking they are getting more pressure on the defender. This will just make it easier for the defender to throw them off because their balance will be off.

The best drill for keeping the feet apart is to use a piece of one-by-twelve-inch lumber about six to ten feet long, and have the lineman drive block against

The drive block is rarely won or lost on the initial hit. It is won by staying low, getting the hands in, and driving the hips. Some players I played against were so strong that you could bounce off them if you put everything into the initial hit. Reggie White is a perfect example of this. He was by far the strongest defensive end I played against. I played against Bruce Clark with the Saints, who was an NCAA weightlifting champion, but for football strength, Reggie was the strongest.

Ed "Too Tall" Jones was another guy that if you tried to blast him you would bounce off. Parcells called him "half time" because he came hard only about half of the time. When he did come he would use his great height (6'9") and hip strength to deliver a tremendous blow. My second game as a pro I learned this, with him actually driving me back into the backfield for the first time in my life. With these types of guys, I would come off the ball a little easier, take on the initial blow, and then work my hands, drive my feet, and work my hips.

a handheld dummy, pushing it down the length of the one-by-twelve. If the blocker does not keep his feet apart, he will slip on the wood and quickly learn not to do this again. For younger players, this drill should be done every day.

The drive block should be taught and practiced in steps. The best tool is the two-man or seven-man sled. I prefer the two-man so that everyone can be observed and corrections made immediately. If you allow players to practice incorrect techniques and do not correct them immediately, the poor technique will become habit and be even harder to change. It is similar to the situation in golf. By the time most golfers go for a lesson, they have so many bad habits that the pro simply tries to work on the most glaring mistakes first. The pro will never be able to get the average golfer to swing totally correctly. This is because the golfer has years of bad habits and muscle memory to overcome. Get your players before they have bad habits or try to correct them every time they do something incorrectly so the muscle memory of proper technique becomes second nature.

First, have them come out of the stance low and hard, taking just the first two steps, and hit a dummy at the correct height with the hands, making sure the head is up, the back is arched, and the hips are in the drive position. The next time through, after proper contact, have them drive the sled up with their hips and lift with their arms to full extension. They should take only the first two steps as in the first part of the drill. The line of their entire body from hands to toes should be slightly curved to the inside toward the sled. Have them maintain this position for two seconds, then have them drop it. In the last part of the drill they hit and lift the sled and keep their feet moving, driving the sled. When they can no longer move the sled, let it drop down and have them continue to drive it for a few more seconds, making sure their heads are up and backs arched.

Drive Blocking a Linebacker

Drive blocking against a linebacker or a player off the line of scrimmage is similar to the basic drive block. You want to come out of your stance low and hard. The first step should be taken with the foot toward the hole. If the hole is right at the linebacker, step with the back foot first. Come up a little with your head on the second and third steps. Just before contact, dip back down to a good hitting position, back arched, head up, neck bowed. Put your forehead on the number to the side of the hole where you expect the back to run. Hit leading with the top of the shoulder pad, getting under his shoulder pads and trying to get your hands on the inside of his chest. The backer will usually try to take you on with a shoulder, trying to get under you, and then use his shoulder and forearm as a flipper to bounce you to one side or the other. Getting your hands on the inside will allow you to control him and stay on the block longer.

Scramble Blocking

Scramble blocking is another type of drive block that is often used by quick-hitting teams. In the scramble block, the blocker drives low at the hip or thigh of the defender (see photo 3.3). He uses the older style of blocking surface in which he grabs his jersey with his hand and uses the surface of his upper and lower arm to contact and control the defender. If he blocks low enough, he can use his other hand to touch the ground and give him a more stable blocking position. Still, even using this technique you will want to get some lift in your block because the opponent's weight you are lifting increases your effective weight (the weight on your feet) and decreases his. So if you get five pounds of the defender's weight on your shoulders or hands it makes him weigh five pounds less and you weigh five pounds more.

As with any block in which your head is to the side of the defender, the rule is to "pinch with the ear and look to the sky." Pinching with your ear helps to keep you in contact with the defender, while looking to the sky helps you to arch your back and get lift on the defender.

Photo 3.3 Scramble block: the blocker drives low at the hip or thigh of the defender

Double-Team, Zone, and Wedge Blocking

Effective teamwork and ability to read the flow of the play are essential for offensive linemen to get their job done, especially in double-team, zone, and wedge blocking.

Double-Team Block

The double-team block starts with two offensive players on one defender (see fig. 4.1 on the next page). When teams ran the single wing, the double-team always kept the two blockers on one defensive man. Today usually one of the offensive players will eventually work off onto another defender, usually a linebacker. Let's use a covered guard and an uncovered tackle as an illustration.

The guard and tackle are responsible for the defensive tackle (DT) over the guard and the linebacker that is lined up over the center. The guard's first step will depend on where the defensive tackle lines up and whether the guard is reading anything from the defensive tackle's stance. If the defensive tackle is on the guard's outside shoulder and the guard does not read that he may try to slant across his face, the step can be with the outside foot, directly at the defender. If the defensive tackle is head up or inside, or he looks like he may slant inside on the snap, then the first step should be with the inside foot, but also straight

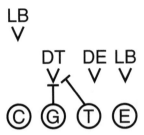

Figure 4.1 Double-team blocking

ahead. The guard must keep an eye on the linebacker over the center, because if the backer runs straight ahead toward the line, the guard is responsible for him and must come off the double-team block and pick up the backer.

After the first step, the block will resemble a drive block. The tackle will come down on the double-team, stepping with his inside foot and aiming for the defensive tackle's outside shoulder and ribcage. Upon contact, he should work his hips toward the guard's hips so there is not a gap that the defender can slide through. Working in tandem, the guard and tackle should drive the defender back and to the inside. The goal is to drive him all the way back into the linebacker. If that is not achieved, both men need to keep an eye on the backer. The general rule is if the backer comes underneath the double-team he belongs to the guard, and if he goes over (behind) the double-team, he belongs to the tackle. The remaining man stays on the defensive tackle.

The defensive tackle has three basic options on how to take on the double-team. First, he can try to split it by lowering his outside shoulder, giving the linemen a smaller area to hit and also giving him a better angle to knife between the linemen. That is why it is essential for the linemen to get their hips together on the block, to not give him a gap to drive through. This is called the *seal*. Second, he can try to beat the man coming down on the block, going across his face to the outside. This is why the man blocking down must aim for the shoulder and ribs of the defender, to not let him get around to the outside. The third option is to go down to the ground and bring both of the blockers down with him. This will create a pile, making it hard for the runner to get a read, and also will allow the backer to go free on the play and make the tackle.

When the tackle comes down on the block, he should hit with his hands and the inside shoulder. If he feels the defender going down, he should push off with his hands so he has the balance to get off the pile and go up on the backer. By using his hands in this way, he will also be in position to push the defensive tackle over to the guard when it is time to go up to the backer.

There are two other types of double-teams. One is the post and pivot (see photo 4.1). In this block the offensive lineman on the defender straightens up the defensive lineman, as in a high drive block. The outside offensive lineman drives into the hips of the defender, driving him down the line of scrimmage. (If the outside lineman were to drive at the knees of the defender it would be an illegal chop block; see photo 4.2.)

Another type of double-team may be used by quick-hitting teams that use scramble blocking (see photo 4.3 on the next page). The two offensive linemen drive low (at about hip or thigh level) with a head on each side of the defender. They seal their shoulders and hips as they scramble block in tandem. This type

Photo 4.1 Post and pivot double-team block: the second lineman drives into the defender's hips

Photo 4.2 An illegal chop block: the lineman drives at the defender's knees

Photo 4.3 Scramble double-team block

of block usually gets the quickest movement on the defender. One blocker, either the inside or the outside man, may come off for the inside backer after a few steps.

In any of the double-teams the coach must be certain that there is a tight seal of the blockers' hips, and, in some blocks, of their shoulders. When you attend practice of a team that uses double-teams you will hear the coach yelling, "Seal, seal!" It is the most critical part of a double-team block.

Another technique that I have had success with on the double-team block is a technique that we called an influence block or a dick block. This is used when a defensive end is lined up slightly off-center of the offensive tackle, slightly to the outside, and the tackle and tight end will be double-teaming him to a backer to the inside (see fig. 4.2). This technique should only be used if the defensive end has quick reactions and is reading heads of the offensive linemen.

The tackle takes a step with his inside foot at a 45-degree angle, like he is going to do a cutoff block for a play going the opposite way. He should then wait slightly for the defender to react, because the defender is taught to try

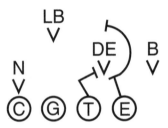

Figure 4.2 Influence or dick block

and fight across the tackle's face to the opposite side. When he makes this move, step up with the outside foot, take your outside arm and slam it into the defender's ribs to keep his momentum going to the inside. The tight end should also come down and give him a push to help drive him across the tackle's face, then go up on the linebacker. This technique can only be used if the end is a fast flow reader, but when they bite on this technique, it can be very effective. The defensive end will end up inside of the tackle, with the tackle between him and the hole. This will stop all flow from the back side. The tight end will have a very easy block getting on the backer, having to give the defensive end a small push before going up.

Zone Blocking

Combination or zone blocking allows the linemen to be aggressive off the line of scrimmage, especially if the defense slants its down linemen. For point-of-attack blocks, this is where a covered and uncovered lineman work together to block the down lineman and the linebacker over the uncovered lineman. For descriptive purposes, we will use an uncovered right guard and a covered right tackle with the point of attack being the guard-tackle gap. The problem being solved by zone blocking is that if the defensive end over the tackle takes an inside move and the linebacker fills in where the tackle was, even if the tackle blocks the defensive end, the guard will not be able to block the linebacker because the defensive end will be in his way.

To solve this, the guard and tackle work together to block the linebacker and defensive end (see fig. 4.3). The tackle can take a hard step with his outside foot and aim for the end's outside number. The guard takes a slide step with his

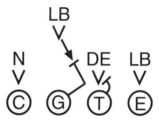

Figure 4.3 Zone block: the defensive end plays head up or slants out

outside foot, being ready to take on the end if he slants to the inside. If the end is playing it straight, his job is to not get hooked, so he will try to work outside when he feels the outside pressure. This then turns into a basic one-on-one drive block. The guard, seeing that the end is not coming inside, should then step up and take on the linebacker as if there was no combination block (see photo 4.4).

If the end does slant to the inside, the block becomes a double-team for a short period of time. The tackle will get a good piece of the end to slow him down, making it easier for the guard to take him over. Once he knows the guard has control of the end, he can then come off the block and come up on the linebacker, who will be trying to fill the hole over the tackle (see fig. 4.4). The tackle must not avoid the end if he is slanting. If he does, the guard will have very little chance of success in blocking the slanting end. This is the error that most often occurs on this type of block. The tackle must get a good piece of the defensive end and turn him over to the guard.

Photo 4.4 Combination or zone blocking: guard takes on the linebacker if the end does not come inside

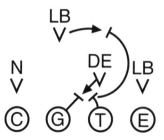

Figure 4.4 Zone block: the defensive end slants in as the linebacker moves to the outside

This block can be used by any two linemen at the point of attack on a straight-ahead dive play, especially if the running back is set deep and is option running—looking for any hole to develop.

This type of block can also be used away from the point of attack (see fig. 4.5). For example, if the right guard is covered and the right tackle has a backer over him and the play is going to the left, the guard and tackle can work in combination on the defensive tackle over the guard and the backer over the offensive tackle. In this situation, since the point of attack is two or three people removed, you will want the offensive tackle to end up on the defensive tackle and the guard to end up on the linebacker. The guard will have a much better angle on the backer than the tackle would. The guard will take a step with his inside foot at a 45- to 60-degree angle, aiming for the inside tip of the shoulder pad of the defensive tackle. How long the guard stays on the block depends on how fast the linebacker is flowing. He should stay on the defensive tackle as long as possible, coming off for the linebacker as late as possible but still making the block.

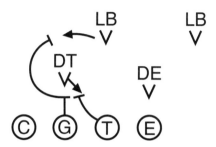

Figure 4.5 Zone block: blocking on the off side away from the point of attack

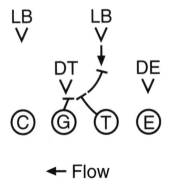

Figure 4.6 Zone offside block when the linebacker is penetrating straight ahead

The offensive tackle will take a flat step, almost like he is pulling (but not gaining depth as when he is in fact pulling), laying his stomach on his thigh. He needs to check on the linebacker out of the corner of his eye, and if the backer is blitzing straight ahead, he needs to stop and block the backer (see fig. 4.6). In this case, the guard will stay on the defensive tackle. If there is no blitz the offensive tackle will continue on, staying low so he gets his head and shoulders in front of the defensive tackle (see fig. 4.7). He should then square up on the defensive tackle and stop him from flowing to the point of attack. If the backer is flowing slowly, the guard and tackle will double-team the defensive tackle until the backer does flow. The only way the guard will not end up on the linebacker is if the defensive tackle is slanting toward the hole. In this case, the guard will cut off the defensive tackle and the offensive tackle will go upfield onto the backer.

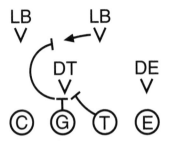

Figure 4.7 Zone offside block when the linebacker goes with the flow

Most coaches teach this rule to the linemen involved in a zone block: "Four hands on the lineman and four eyes on the backer."

Wedge Block

The wedge block is a team block that is often used near the goal line or in short-yardage situations. The block is generally done on a defensive lineman rather than a linebacker. The offensive blocker on that lineman works to get under him and stand him up. It is just the same as a drive block. The linemen on each side of the blocker block the back of the blocker's hips, helping him drive the defensive lineman backward (see photo 4.5). The wedge can be a three- or a five-man block.

Photo 4.5 Wedge block

$$\boxed{5}$$

Cross and Fold Blocking

C ross blocks and fold blocks are blocking adjustments in which the linemen who would normally block the man over them exchange assignments. Most coaches will call it a *cross block* if both men block defenders who are on the line of scrimmage and a *fold block* if one blocks a defensive lineman and the other blocks a linebacker.

Cross Block

The cross block is used to block two adjacent linemen. Let's assume that the team is playing a true Okie 5-2: there is a defensive tackle on the offensive tackle and a defensive end outside the offensive end. In this case the offensive end blocks down on the defensive tackle and the offensive tackle steps to the side and blocks the defensive end or a stand up linebacker (see fig. 5.1 on the next page). In photo 5.1, I am pulling around the down block by the tight end and coming around on the outside backer. I am trying to hook him if possible on this play, but odds are that the back will cut up under my block if the backer flows too strong to the outside.

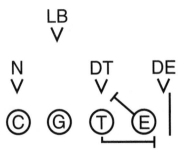

Figure 5.1 Cross block between tackle and end

Fold Block

A fold block, sometimes called a doodad block, is where you have one covered and one uncovered lineman and you are running a straight-ahead play and want to change the blocking scheme. The uncovered lineman will block the man over the covered lineman, and the covered lineman will circle around and up and block the backer over the uncovered lineman. For example let's use a tackle covered by a defensive end and an uncovered guard (see fig. 5.2). The guard will block out on the defensive end, similar to the down block described in the next chapter. Since this is a point-of-attack block, he should stay up and not use the crab stance.

The tackle will take a pull-type step, gaining depth to get around the guard. Once he clears the guard, he should immediately turn upfield and take on the backer with his head to the outside, creating a crease between the backer and end for the back to run through. The back will have only one read, to run into

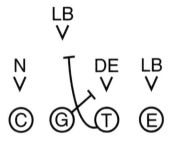

Figure 5.2 Fold between guard and tackle

Photo 5.1 Cross block

Credit: Jerry Pinkus

the crease created by the cross block. There will not be cutback lanes available. Also, if the guard sees that the backer is threatening to blitz straight ahead, he needs to call off the cross block because the backer will probably beat the tackle to the hole and be in the backfield before he can be blocked. Likewise, if the tackle can determine that the defensive end is slanting to the outside, he should call off the cross block because the guard will not be able to get to him and it will be a very easy block for the tackle. The call should change to a scoop block where the tackle hits the slanting defensive end, lets the guard, who is taking a step toward him, take over the defensive end, and the tackle goes up on the backer (see fig. 5.3). It is important that the back hears the changed blocking call since it will greatly affect his read.

The block out by the guard is essentially a down block, only it is done to the outside. The guard will step with his outside foot, pointing it at the hand of the man he is blocking out on. He needs to gain as much distance with this step as he can so as to get on the defensive end as quickly as possible. The guard's head should be aimed at the crease of the neck and shoulder of the defensive end. Upfield penetration is not as much a concern in the out block because the back will run inside of this block and penetration by the defensive end will not affect other blockers as it may with linemen pulling around a down block. The inside hand should aim for the hip of the defensive end. This is a point-of-attack block, so any sideways movement that can be generated will help the play. Even letting the man get upfield will create a crease for the back to see and run through.

The tackle should take a drop step to the inside like he is pulling, throwing his inside elbow back and keeping his upper body low. This is to give the guard room to make the out block. After one small step with the outside foot to clear

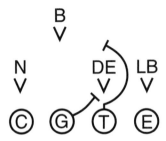

Figure 5.3 Scoop block

the guard, the tackle will pivot on his inside foot and turn upfield and block the backer. When the offensive tackle sees the block by the guard, he should take an outside move and go upfield. It is important for the tackle to come around the guard as closely as possible to get a good angle on the backer. He should try to knock the backer to the inside, creating the natural hole for the back. If the tackle rounds his approach to the backer too much, with the backer already moving to the outside, it will be impossible to get an outside in block on him, so he cannot be driven to the inside, as the play is designed to do. By staying tight, the tackle will hit the backer, aiming his head at the outside shoulder of the backer, with an inside out angle, allowing him to drive the backer to the inside.

Drill

To get the feel of how the tackle should come around the guard, have the tackle line up next to an upright blocking dummy replicating where the guard would be. On the snap the tackle should take his drop step, take the small step with his outside foot, and then turn up on the other side of the dummy. Emphasize staying close to the dummy, even putting his inside hand on it to feel his way around, then turn up. A second bag, replicating the backer, originally lined up over the guard, should be moved up and over at the snap. The tackle should pull up and hit the dummy with his head on the outside and drive it to the inside (see fig. 5.4).

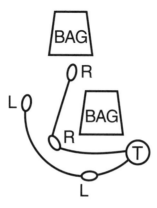

Figure 5.4 Drill for fold block

$$\boxed{6}$$

Down, Reach, and Cutoff Blocks

I t would be simple to teach who to block if the defender always lined up directly in front of you, but that is not the case. Defenders to be blocked may be in either gap or on the man to either side of you. Moving to make such blocks requires additional techniques.

The down block (blocking a man away from the hole), a reach block (blocking a man toward the hole), or a cutoff block (merely preventing a man away from the hole from pursuing effectively) all need to be mastered by effective blockers.

Down Block (Blocking One Man Away)

A down block is used when a man who is supposed to pull is covered and the person in the direction that he is pulling is not covered. This can be when a guard has to pull to the outside and he is covered and the tackle is not covered. The tackle blocks down on the man over the guard (see fig. 6.1 on the next page). This can be a tough block, depending on how the defender plays it. If the guard pulls and the defender fires hard upfield, he can get right behind the guard and make the play on the back who is trying to follow the guard. If the

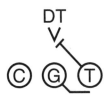

Figure 6.1 Down block by tackle

defender reads the play quickly, he may try to fight the down block by gaining a little depth and going behind the down block. This is why it is important for the guard not to tip that he is pulling.

Two basic techniques can be used for this block. The most basic is for the tackle to step down hard with his inside foot at a 30- to 45-degree angle, staying low by laying his stomach on his thigh. He should aim his head for the defender's far hip or shoulder, getting his head between the man and the line of scrimmage. This is to stop the hard upfield move penetrating into the offensive backfield. Deliver a blow with the outside shoulder into the defender's rib area, making sure that your outside hand is up and aimed for the defender's hip (see photo 6.1). This is to stop the outside move. If the defender tries to go upfield, the second step should continue down the line of scrimmage to stop penetration. If the defender's move is to the outside, the second step should be upfield, swinging the hips to a 90-degree angle with the line of scrimmage, creating as big a surface as possible to stop the man from getting to the sideline.

The other technique is a crab technique or low reverse shoulder block. With this, the blocker will step almost flat down the line of scrimmage with his inside foot while throwing his outside arm across the defender to stop the upfield move,

Photo 6.1 Down block

Against the Washington Redskins, who played a 4-3 defense, a good part of the time when we ran the ball to the outside, I had to down block on Dave Butts. Dave is a huge person, about 6'4", and he was over three hundred pounds. This was when there were few three hundred–pounders in the league. Knowing that we did a lot of down blocking, he was always looking out of the corner of his eye for me to come down. He wasn't quick enough to get upfield on me, but he fought like hell to get through me. I have a picture that a friend gave to me showing me down blocking on Dave, and he had his hand grabbing the bottom of my face mask trying to rip my head off by pushing it back. The following year he did the same thing to me, and I screamed at him to get his hand off my face mask. He said that he was sorry and didn't mean to, but I came right back and said I had a picture of him doing it to me the year before so I knew he meant to (see photo 6.2). He didn't say anything back after that, and he did keep his hands off my mask the rest of the day.

Photo 6.2 Down block on Dave Butts

Credit: Jerry Pinkus

ending up with both hands on the ground. Once you cut him off, swing your outside leg upfield as far as possible, turning your body so that it is at a 90-degree angle with the line of scrimmage with your head toward the line of scrimmage. You should be on all fours with your hips fighting to stay between the defender and the sideline.

The first option, staying up, is generally preferred because it will allow adjustments to the defender's moves to be easier (see photos 6.3 and 6.4). It is also more athletic. The other problem is that the crab position exposes the lineman's ribs and he is susceptible to a cheap shot to the ribs.

By getting a pre-snap read on the defender, you can know which way he may be going. If he has a lot of weight on his hand, he is more likely to go upfield, and if his weight is back in his stance he is more likely to try to fight across your face to get to the outside. You can also see if the defender is reading the puller or you. This is where film study is extremely valuable; if you can know ahead of time how the defense will fight the down block, you can adjust your technique to fit the expected defensive technique.

Photo 6.3 Reach block

Photo 6.4 Scramble reach or down block (also called a reverse shoulder block)

Reach Block

A reach block is when the blocker has to block a man that is either in the gap or lined up on the blocker next to him toward where the play is going (see fig. 6.2). The reason the blocker to the play side is not taking this man is because he has another responsibility, which is probably pulling to the play side, which will influence the defender to go with him. A textbook reach block will have the blocker not only work his way into the face of the defender, but actually hook him and stop him from flowing to the hole. In practical terms, this is almost impossible unless the defense is slanting to the blocker or the defender is not very good. In photo 6.5 on the next page, the center, Bart Oates, has completed a reach block on the man that was lined up over the guard. On this play, I came down to help him and then went up on the back side backer.

The biggest thing that has to be defended against is penetration by the man being reached. If he gets penetration, he will follow the blocker that pulled toward the play and no one will be there to block him. The lineman needs to have his first step be a pull-type step with the foot toward the direction of the play. For a reach to the right, he will take the drop step with his right foot, throwing his right elbow back to get turned to the right. His second step will also be to the right, but on the third step he needs to make contact with the defender, turning into him and getting his hands on him as quickly as he can. You do want to try to face up the man if possible. The important thing is to get your hands on him and deter him from running freely to the play. Since a reach block is not a block called for near the point of attack, there will be quite some

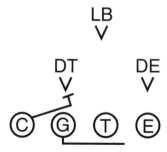

Figure 6.2 Reach block by center

Photo 6.5 Reach block on a linebacker   *Credit: Jerry Pinkus*

The San Francisco 49ers used the clip technique mentioned on page 45 in the 1980s and 1990s. Everyone in the league hated them for doing it. Many cheap shots were taken against their players because of this technique. The Giants' defensive players would talk to us and encourage us to try to hurt their guys because they saw the 49ers' tactics as trying to hurt them. There are times during a game where you have a defensive player in a compromising position where he can get hurt. Against any other team I would do my best to pull up and not hurt the defender, hoping that he would do the same for me, but I had a harder time doing this for the 49ers, knowing what they were trying to do to the Giants' defensive linemen. Fortunately, no one got hurt on either team while I was playing. I like to see football as an honorable game where you go out and do your best to beat the other team and legally knock the heck out of the other team, but I couldn't look the other team in the eye at the end of the game if I knew a technique we were using had a very high chance of hurting one of the opponents.

distance between where this block starts and where the play is. There will probably be many other players, both offensive and defensive, in between, and you can try to run the defender into the other players. If this is not possible, just keeping contact and running with him should be sufficient.

There is another technique available for this type of block, but I strongly recommend that it not be used. It takes advantage of the rule that it is legal to clip within the "tackle box," from tackle to tackle, if the defender has lined up on the line of scrimmage. (Under the new high school rules it is not legal to clip a linebacker—only a lineman lined up within four yards of the center.) With this legal clip, the reach-blocking lineman dives into the back of the defender's legs as he is running toward the play. This is legal, but highly dangerous, and not necessary if the blocker uses good technique and effort. I see it as a lazy and cheap way of blocking.

Cutoff Block

A cutoff block is used when you want to "cut off" a defender from getting to the play. This block is usually described as a back-side block, meaning it is on the back side of the play. If your offense uses cutback-type reads by the running back, the cutoff block is often the most important block on the play. Often, on a read play, the hole that develops is not on the front side, but is created when the defense overpursues and one blocker gets a good cutoff block, creating a huge hole in the defense.

The block starts with the lineman stepping with the foot toward where the hole is. The step should be at a 45-degree angle. You want your aiming point to be the armpit of the defender. The hands should go toward the play side of the defender, with the inside hand trying to get in the defender's armpit. This will allow better control of the man. The second step will also be at the same 45-degree angle. The third step should be upfield while turning your body to face the defender and your back to the hole. It is very easy just to get body-to-body with the defender and move down the line of scrimmage with him, but this will not give the back the cutback read he is looking for. This is as much an "effort and attitude" block as a drive block.

Blockers often try to use a scramble cutoff block where they attempt to dive at the play-side leg of the defender and cut him to the ground. This rarely, if ever, works. The defender simply pushes the blocker down with his hands, steps over him, and goes down the line of scrimmage, not allowing the cutback lane that the back is looking for. The blocker thinks that since this is a back-side block and is not at the point of attack, the block is not important. Diving at the feet of the defender takes very little energy and effort and is the "easy way" out of blocking. If it were successful, I would be all for it since you want the easiest way of making a block, but it is rarely successful. The only time it should be considered is if you are running a goal line or short-yardage play to the other side and the defender tips that he is taking a hard inside move. Here, since there are a lot of bodies between the blocker and the point where the back is looking to run, and he is not looking for a cutback lane, this block will be fine.

If the play is a sweep to the opposite side, the cutoff block is not as important, but it is a great opportunity for the blocker to make a downfield block to greatly help the play. The downfield release can only be done if the defender does not have the speed to run down the play from the back side. If the blocker is faster than the defender, you should be fine. The block is more of a release than a block. Take a hard step to the side of the play with the inside foot at a 30-degree angle with the line of scrimmage. The hands should come up and into the armpit area of the defender. The second step should be hard upfield. At this time push the defender to the outside with both arms, making sure you go between the defender and where the ball is going to be run.

I was able to do cutoff blocks often in college, and it is one of the reasons that I stood out in the scouts' eyes when they came to look at me for the pros. It is also how I got the attention of the coaches with the Giants. We were playing the Patriots in the first preseason game in 1984, my second rookie season after being on injured reserve my first year in 1983. I was the starter at right tackle, but by no means did I have the job secured. We ran a number of sweeps to the left, and I cut my man off and made three or four blocks downfield. Bill Belichick, who was then our defensive coordinator, came up to me after he saw the films and complimented me on those blocks and asked why didn't I show them I could do that before. I just said that I hadn't had the opportunity to do it before. This was a defensive coach saying this to me, so I knew all the offensive coaches noticed.

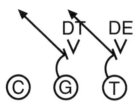

Figure 6.3 Cutoff blocks and downfield release

Once you are past the defender, take a flat 30-degree angle toward the opposite sideline, looking at where the back is and then upfield to see who you can block (see fig. 6.3). Usually this will be the back-side safety or cornerback. This is a full-effort block and means running at full speed for about twenty to thirty yards and then getting under control to make the block on a little defensive back, but there is nothing prettier than seeing a big guy lead the back downfield and make the block to spring the ball carrier into the end zone. Rosie Brown, who was a Hall of Fame tackle for the Giants in the 1950s, was one of the first athletic tackles who was able to do this block consistently, and he got into the Hall of Fame because of it.

7

Pulling and Trapping

In most offenses linemen are required to trap on some plays or to pull through the line on the play side or to pull in counter plays to the back side. They may also be called on to pull to protect a passer who is rolling out, bootlegging, or roving (a planned roll after a drop back). While the initial pulling action is somewhat similar in each case, the ultimate blocking assignment may be quite different.

The Initial Steps

Pulling from the same stance you use to drive block and pass protect from is not an easy thing to do and will take much practice to do properly (see photo 7.1 on the next page). For a right-handed player pulling to the left, the moves that get you going are pushing off with your right or down hand while taking your left elbow and throwing it backward, as hard as you can, to get the body moving backward and turned to the left (see fig. 7.1). The left elbow will be pulled back near the back of the left hip as the left leg steps sideward. While turning, the left foot should drop back about six to twelve inches and turn so that it is pointing in the direction you want to go.

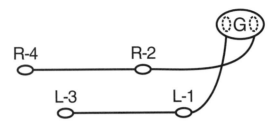

Figure 7.1 Pull left

You need to get some depth on this first step to clear the person immediately to your left. As you turn keep your upper body low, trying to put your stomach and chest on your left thigh. As you turn and step with your left leg your right hand should be thrown forward to help get you turned. It will also help you to get into your running coordination quickly, with the left leg and right arm both moving forward at the same time.

The most common mistake pullers make is to false step or step up with the right foot to start to turn. This creates an extra step that will make you one step slower getting to the hole. The other error is that the lineman will jump up with both feet from the stance and turn his body while in the air toward the direction he is pulling and then start to run. The problem with this is that you still have to take a step back to clear the man to your left. This would require an extra step. Also you tend to stand straight up, which gets you out of your stance more slowly. Getting to the point of attack as quickly as possible is the key to pulling. If it takes too long to get out of your stance and get going, then the defense has more time to react and the play is probably doomed to fail.

For a right-handed player pulling to the right, the same keys apply. You will throw your down hand and elbow back hard to get your body turned (see photo 7.2). The right foot is back already so it is more of a pivot than a step. You don't

Photo 7.1 Pull to left

have to get as much depth with this step since this foot was back to begin with. Lay the chest and stomach on the right thigh, throw the left hand in the direction you want to go, and run to the point of attack. You may want to put a hand on the man next to you so you can feel your way around him and not trip on him. If you do this, it must be a light touch, not enough to knock your own man off-balance and off his block.

Photo 7.2 Pull to right

The Short Trap

A trap—originally called a *mousetrap*—is a play in which the defender is coaxed to come across the line looking for a wide play, then he is blocked out and the play run inside of him. For a short trap block, such as a guard blocking the man over the tight end, you should stay low the whole time until contact, not standing up and then dipping down to make contact, trying to get under the man. Stay as close as you can to the line of scrimmage without tripping on your own players' legs. The man you are blocking will probably be coming upfield and turning in. He will be looking into the backfield and see action toward him so he should be expecting either the guard pulling or a lead back coming out on him. Usually, this person's job is to keep outside containment and force the play inside. He will generally lower his inside shoulder and try to take you on with his shoulder and arm acting as a flipper. He will try to squeeze down the hole by coming inside. The guard's job is to root him out of the hole. This is done by coming in low and hard, aiming for his ribcage with your upfield shoulder, and running through the man, moving him to the outside. Lead with your shoulder, but get your hands on him as well, aiming for his hip and chest wall with the hands to help control him and give him the final push out of the hole. If you aim too much at his shoulder or head, he may spin back to the inside, closing the hole. If you aim too far toward his back side, he may run around the block and still make the play. If the player is making a hard move upfield, you may not be able to get a hard hit on him, but just a push should be enough to keep him out of the play. If he has gone too far upfield and run himself out of the play, just turn up the hole and become an extra blocker.

The Long Trap

A longer trap block can occur if you are pulling the back-side guard to trap a man over the strong side tight end. With a longer trap, you will not be able to stay low for the entire time before the trap occurs. In order to run athletically, you will have to be more upright. The lower you can stay, the better off you will be, but you must be up enough to run athletically and efficiently. It is still important to come out of your stance low and hard for the first step, then you can rise up. Once again, run as close behind your fellow blockers as you can without tripping on them. Since you are pulling for a slightly longer period, the man you will be blocking will have a better chance of being ready to take you on and have more time to close down the hole. Just before contact, you will need to get low, because, as always, the low man wins. The same aiming point should be used as for the short trap.

Adjusting to the Situation: The Log Block

There are situations where a trap block is called for but the defense will not allow it. If the man being trapped does not have outside contain or was slanting to the inside, no matter how hard you try to root him out of the hole, you will not be able to. He will have too much momentum coming down or may be too far inside for there to be a hole. In this case, the puller must make a quick decision and execute a log block.

A log block is a block made by a pulling lineman or a lead back in which the blocker gets to the outside of the defender and the play goes outside of him. It looks like a trap block to begin with but ends with the opposite effect on the defender (the play goes outside instead of inside). Instead of trapping the man, you pin him inside and the back has to adjust and take the play outside.

If the guard reads that a trap is impossible, then his aiming point must change to the point of the shoulder of the defender. You will make contact with your inside (left if pulling to the right) shoulder, and upon contact swing your

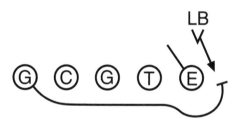

Figure 7.2 Log block

hips around to the outside and pin the man to the inside. Your inside hand should get him below his shoulder. This will help slow you down so you can spin around on the log block and stop him from going under you to make a play. The upfield arm will then come around and control him from going to the outside. As you do this, your inside hand needs to come around to join the upfield hand so that you do not grab the defender and get called for holding. This becomes more of a position block than a drive block. Knowing the defense's tendencies can greatly help this situation. Also having a call made by a front-side lineman if he reads a slant to the inside will alert both the puller and the back of a potential log block situation.

You may also have plays designed to go outside where you want the puller to log block the outside man on the line of scrimmage (see fig. 7.2). In this case, the puller should take the same path as if he is going to trap, making the defender play the trap block. With his weight to the inside to take on the trap, it will be easier to log him to the inside. With about two steps to go before contact, start to belly back to get position for the log block, now aiming for the tip of his upfield shoulder instead of his ribcage. If you show the log block too soon, the man will work upfield and force both you and the back to go deep, which will destroy the play.

Working with the Fullback

If the guard is pulling outside for a safety or corner and the fullback is blocking the outside man on the line of scrimmage, the guard can help the fullback by taking the first couple of steps like he is going to trap the end man. This will cause the end man to have his weight to the inside, making the fullback's block easier. After the first couple of steps, you will have to belly or swerve back away from the line of scrimmage to clear the fullback's block.

Pulling for a Downfield Block

After clearing the fullback's block, the pulling lineman has to block either the corner or strong safety, whoever has force on the play. This sounds like a lineman's dream, going out to plow over a little defensive back. The only problem is hitting that little person. The puller must stay under control, shortening the length of his strides and getting some width to his feet as he gets closer to the defensive back. (In photo 7.3, I have just turned up into the hole and am starting to breakdown to hit the safety. I got a great hit on him, putting him on the ground, and the play picked up about 15 yards.) At this point a read must be made. The defensive back has three options. The first is to take the block on like a linebacker, high and hard, and try to squeeze down the hole from the outside in. If this is the case, take the defensive back on like a linebacker, maintaining the inside out control of him by hitting him in the ribcage, aiming between his shoulders and hips. Get your hands in and on his body as you make contact to control him. This will drive the man outside and give the back a great read to cut the ball back up.

The second option is for the defensive back to come up and try to use his quickness to avoid the blocker and still make the play. This is why the puller must stay in control as he comes out on the block. To make your blocking surface as big as possible, you can use a cross body type of block. For example, if pulling to the right to hit a defensive back, as you get within a step of the defensive back you would throw your left arm, keeping it extended, at his upfield shoulder while throwing your hips and legs behind the man, bending your left leg up to help trap him in your body. The block must be made at the waist or above to prevent a penalty. This is a risky block because if you miss, you will look like a fool, but it will give you the largest hitting area to make the block on a moving and evasive target. The other option is to stay up high and try to get your hands on the man. While doing this, be sure to maintain an inside out position on the man so the back has a lane to cut up underneath your block.

The third option for the defensive back is to come up hard and hit you low, creating a pile deep in the backfield that the back has to adjust around. There

Photo 7.3 Preparing for a downfield block

Credit: Jerry Pinkus

is not a lot that you can do here except go low and blast him so hard that he will not want to do that again in the future.

Knowing your opponent and his tendencies will greatly help you in knowing what to expect when you come out on your block. Ronnie Lott would like to come up and take on the blocker like a linebacker, while Deion Sanders would do his best to avoid contact and dance around blocks.

Pulling to Block the Backer

There will be times when the uncovered lineman will pull, but it will not be a trapping situation. You can have a basic man-on-man blocking scheme for an outside run where an uncovered guard or center is to block the backer over him. If he tries to go through the line to get him, he would have to go upfield to avoid the man over the tackle, but this angle would not let him get the fast-flowing backer. In this case, the guard would pull to the outside, but it would be to block the man originally over him. The guard would take the first three steps like he was pulling, but after that he needs to keep an eye on the backer. If the backer tries to run through the hole the guard created by pulling, the guard must react, stop, and come back to make the block on the backer since he is responsible for him no matter where he goes (see fig. 7.3). If the backer flows to the outside, then the guard continues to the outside looking for a hole to go up and block the backer (see fig. 7.4). The guard should stay slightly behind the backer as they both flow outside because the back is looking for a cutback hole. When a hole does appear, it will appear to the backer as well as the back. The guard must read this and get up in the hole and block the backer, giving the back a clear read on the run.

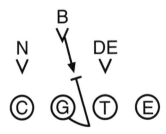

Figure 7.3 Pulling to block the linebacker who is filling the hole

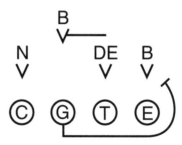

Figure 7.4 Pulling to block the linebacker who is flowing

Pulling on the Bootleg

Pulling on a bootleg presents a different problem and approach. The flow of the play is going the opposite direction from where the quarterback is rolling. The lead blocker, either guard or the center, will pull opposite of the flow to lead the quarterback to the outside (see fig. 7.5). When the pull is made, even though it is a long pull, you want to stay as low as possible for the first few steps so as not to give away the play to the defense. The job of the puller will be to log in the outside man on the line so the quarterback can break containment. The

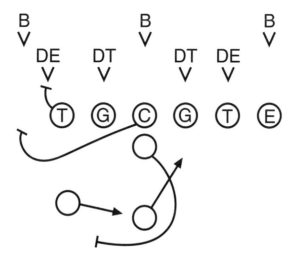

Figure 7.5 Pulling on the bootleg

play is designed so the man being blocked by the puller will read flow away and come flat down the line. If the last man on the line drops off in coverage, then the puller is a personal escort for the quarterback, blocking anyone who comes up from the secondary or turning back to get anyone who may have leaked from the inside. If no one is open, he needs to listen to the quarterback to say "Go," and then he can go downfield and be a lead blocker for the quarterback on a run.

Pulling for the Quick Screen

A lineman can also pull on a wide quick screen where the defensive back is off the wide receiver, the quarterback takes one step back and fires the ball out to the wideout. The pulling lineman, usually a tackle in this case, must pull and sprint out to block the defensive back who has coverage on the wideout before he can come up and make the play (see fig. 7.6). The puller will want to keep inside out position on the defensive back as he goes out, and then block the defensive back as described earlier.

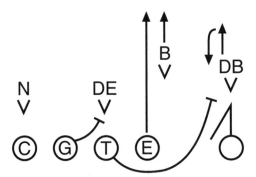

Figure 7.6 Pulling for the quick screen to the wideout

8

Blocking on the Goal Line

hile watching a football game on TV or listening to it on the radio, how often have you heard that a goal line or short-yardage play didn't work because the offensive line didn't get any push? I hear it all the time and it ticks me off. With the defensive line charging low and hard, you are happy just to create a pile!

Most of the time, the play on the goal line or short yardage is made by a backer, and usually by the back-side backer. He is the hardest man to block on this type of play.

In a goal line situation, the linemen take very tight splits, usually about six inches. This is to stop a defensive lineman from shooting a gap and getting through the line of scrimmage clean to make the play. Normally, the goal line defense will be a variation on a 6-2, with defensive tackles in the two center-guard gaps. The defensive ends will line up on the tackles, and outside backers with their hands down will line up on the tight ends (see fig. 8.1 on the next page). The defensive linemen will be in four-point stances with their heads low and their butts high. They will be trying to get under the offensive linemen and drive them back.

With the defensive linemen this low, there is very little you can do with them. The offensive linemen will also be low in their stances. A four-point stance is acceptable here if they are comfortable with it. If not, a three-point stance will still be fine, but have the linemen bend their elbows more and have

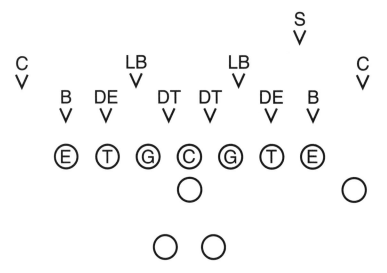

Figure 8.1 6-5 goal line defense

them put their hands out farther in front of them to be lower in their stance. They should line up as close as possible to the line of scrimmage so they can at least maintain that line.

On a straight dive type of play on the goal line, generally there are seven offensive linemen (center, two guards, two tackles, and two tight ends) and six down defensive linemen as described earlier. With two backs in the backfield, there will generally be a lead blocker for the front-side backer. The two tackles and tight ends are covered and will have one-on-one blocks with the men over them. That leaves the center and two guards to block the two men in the gaps and the backside linebacker. The tackles and tight ends have the "easy" blocks. They want to come out low and hard into the defenders, trying to get under them and push them back as with a normal drive block. The head must stay up during this block because often the linemen will be slanting and the blockers need to stay with them. If you can get your hands in on the defender's chest it is a plus, but with the man going low, it will be very difficult to do this. The block is not one in which you will both be in an up position where you have to control your man for a long period of time.

Knowing the point of attack is a great advantage. If you believe that the man over a lineman may be slanting, play to hit the man a little to the side the ball is being run to. If he slants that way, just continue to ride him down in that direction. If he slants the other way, unless he is an incredible athlete, he will not be able to react back and make the play. If he plays straight, you have inside out position on him.

If the lineman tries to submarine under the blocker, the defenders are taught to come up after this and grasp for any movement such as a ball carrier's legs or even pulling a lineman's leg. Generally the opposing linemen just hit each other with very little movement gained by either side. The offensive linemen need to keep their feet moving, not leaving them out behind themselves. If they hit and leave their feet back they can trip any pulling offensive players or the ball carrier. Also, by having their feet closer to the line, they will allow the back, if he is going to jump over the pile, to be closer to the line when he makes his jump.

Now back to that back-side backer. The classic theory on getting him is to have the front-side guard and center double-team the defensive tackle in the front-side gap and drive him back into the back-side backer. If you have two studs blocking and a weak player against them, this may work, but it didn't work often in the pros. When the defensive tackle reads the double-team, he will just go to the ground, creating a huge pileup and not allowing either the guard or center to come off on the backer. The main job of the defensive tackles, besides not getting moved, is to keep the backers clean from blockers.

One technique that can be successful is to have either the front-side guard or the center jump over the defensive tackle to get to the backer. You will not get a great block on him, but all you need in this instance is to get in his way so that he will not have a full-speed hit on the ball carrier. It can look kind of funny, like a salmon jumping up a waterfall to get upstream, but it can work. Which man jumps depends on how the defensive tackle is playing. There are

I mentioned in Chapter 3 that I moved one of the best run stoppers on a goal line play and that really impressed Coach Parcells. Well, that doesn't happen very often. Usually you just get stalemates on the line. It is unreasonable to expect movement every time, but you don't have to let your players know that.

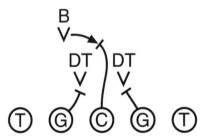

Figure 8.2 Center jumps over defensive tackle to block the linebacker

three positions for him: play straight, slant to the inside, or slant to the outside. If the linemen can read a slant to the outside, then the center will have the easiest job of making the jump block with the guard taking on the defensive tackle (see fig. 8.2). If he is slanting inside, the guard will jump, leaving the center with a reach block for the man in the gap (see fig. 8.3). If he plays straight up, usually the center will be the jumper on a play that hits over the guard and the guard will be the jumper if the play is hitting any wider than that.

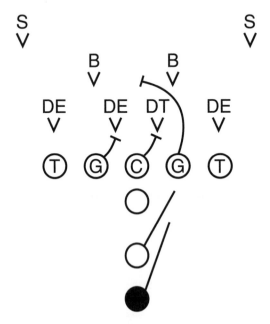

Figure 8.3 Guard jumps over defensive tackle to block the linebacker

On a play over the guard you want a solid block on the defensive tackle, and this will be easier for the guard, who will be blocking slightly down on him. The backer will not be flowing as fast, which will allow the center to get on him. On a wider play, the block on the defensive tackle is not as critical, so a reach block by the center should work, and the backer will be flowing faster, giving the guard an easier block on the jump.

On a play going off tackle, the front-side guard is generally pulled. The center will do a reach block on the defensive tackle in the front-side gap. The tackle will drive block the defensive end over him. The tight end and wingback will double-team the outside backer over the tight end and work to pick up the backside backer. The lead back will block out on the man with outside contain. The front-side guard will pull, turn up into the hole created, and block the front-side backer. When the guard pulls, he needs to be conscious of the legs of his linemen, so as not to trip. They may not be getting as much movement near the goal line as they might in midfield. As he is pulling, the guard's instinct will be to see the man who has containment and want to block him. He has to fight this instinct because this man will be blocked by the lead back (see fig. 8.4). As soon as he finds a hole, he needs to turn up and be ready to block the backer. The backer will be filling hard when he reads the play. Once again, you don't need a kill shot on him, just enough to get the back into the end zone. Hit him as low as you can while being in control, aiming for his chest. Hand control is

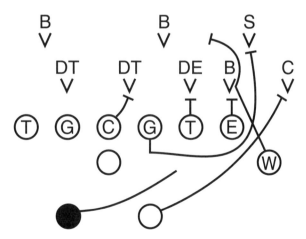

Figure 8.4 Off-tackle play on the goal line

not as important since it will not be a block you will have to hold for an extended period of time.

On a sweep, the front-side guard will also be asked to pull. On this pull, he will be picking up the outside containment person. The key to this play is to give the back a read as quickly as possible. If the guard can log this man to the inside, the back should have a walk-in touchdown. This may be possible if the defender is coming hard to the inside, overplaying an inside move. If the man is playing his job correctly, keeping outside containment, then the guard should try to drive him out, giving the back a hole to run to the inside.

9

Drop Back Pass Protection

Most coaches believe that the most important part of the passing attack is the offensive line. Receivers are second, and the quarterback is third. This is a different hierarchy than what most fans think, more often ranking them quarterback, receivers, and offensive linemen.

Pass protection is a very easy concept. All you have to do is stop a group of defenders from getting to the quarterback for about three and a half seconds. It is essentially playing defense in basketball, only you can use your hands. The thing that makes it tough is that the defensive man can also use his hands. Because of the basketball-like nature of pass blocking, linemen should be encouraged to play a great deal of basketball to get better with their hands and feet. It will help develop quick feet, particularly if they play good defense against quick offensive players.

The basics of pass protection are the same for all offensive line positions, but each position has slight differences based upon where the quarterback will set up the initial movements.

The Initial Movements

First, the basics. While pass protecting, the head should be kept back. This will help keep balance. If the head is down or too far forward, then the weight is

You can have the greatest quarterback in the world and have the greatest receivers in the world, but if the quarterback does not have enough time to throw, it is all meaningless. Kerry Collins, for his time with the Giants, was an exceptional quarterback as long as he had time to throw the ball. If he was rushed or had to move in the pocket at all, his efficiency went down greatly. In Super Bowl XXXV, when the Giants played the Baltimore Ravens and their great defense, Kerry Collins and the Giants offense looked like a bad Pop Warner team. On the first offensive play, Collins threw a pass as a check down to the tight end, but because he was rushed the pass was almost intercepted. This was about the safest pass they had in the playbook, and it was destroyed by the pass rush.

The rest of the day, the Giants looked like they were "trying" plays rather than attacking with an offensive game plan because they did not get the time to throw the ball. Very average quarterbacks can win in the NFL if they are given time. In that same Super Bowl, the Ravens offense was led by Trent Dilfer. The Ravens thought enough of him to not invite him back the next year, even though he "led" them to a Super Bowl victory. They were predominately a run team, but when they had to throw, he had time and got the job done well enough to win.

forward, and the slightest mistake will cause the lineman to fall forward, allowing the defender to get around him. Similarly, the shoulders should be kept back and the back straight or slightly arched. The knees should be bent in a good football position—about 30 degrees from being straight, and the feet should be about shoulder width or slightly wider apart, also for balance. In case you hadn't noticed, balance is very important to pass protection! It is by far the most important thing, because all of pass rushing is predicated on getting the offensive lineman off-balance. In photo 9.1, I have gotten out of my stance with my head back and inside arm up to stop the inside move. My outside arm will come up as the defender comes closer.

The arms should be fully extended, keeping the defender as far away as possible (see photo 9.2 on the next page). The farther away he is, the more time you have to react to what he is doing, allowing you more time to recover. If you are body-to-body with the defender, the slightest advantage gained by the defender

Photo 9.1 Set for pass protection   *Credit: Jerry Pinkus*

will allow him success in getting around you. With the arms at full extension, the hands should be on the defender's chest, with your hands inside those of the defender. Do not grab cloth. This is illegal and is only a crutch for those who are not good enough to do it legally. The thumbs should be turned up. This will force your arms to be straighter and your shoulders to stay back. I have found this little tip to be very helpful with younger players. The feet should be moved in short, choppy steps, always keeping one foot on the ground. The player's weight should be balanced between the heel and toe of the foot. If a player is

Photo 9.2 Pass protection stance

on his toes too much before contact with the rusher or while he is trying a move, he will tend to have too much weight forward and be off-balance. He should only go up on his toes once he has to stop the forward momentum of the rusher.

Some people think pass protection is a passive type of block. In some ways it is, because you have to react to the rusher. If you go out to hit him and miss, you can get your quarterback killed. But if you use good technique, staying in front of the rusher, and get pushed back into the quarterback, you have not done your job either. The quarterback will feel the pressure and want to get rid of the ball too quickly, or he will have to move in the pocket, giving other rushers a better chance for a sack because the linemen will no longer be protecting the proper spot. Knowing where the quarterback is will tell the lineman when he has to make his stand and stop giving ground. At some point, if the lineman is doing his job, the pass rusher will stop trying various moves and go to a bull or power rush. This is where you make your stand and stop giving ground, getting up on your toes and pushing back.

You can and should deliver a blow or punch with your hands while pass protecting. The punch, though, has to be delivered without putting weight forward. You do not want to lunge into the blow. If possible you want to time the blow so that your arms reach full extension just as you make contact with the rusher's chest. This is a situation where you do not want to hit at a point six inches behind your actual target, as it might be in a drive block. If contact is made just as you lock out your elbows, there will be some forward force to the blow, but it will feel like hitting the butt end of a two-by-four for the rusher because his momentum into you will deliver the rest of the blow.

The player with the best punch I ever saw was Tunch "the Punch" Ilkin, a tackle for the Steelers in the 1980s. His timing was incredible. He timed nearly every punch perfectly, being fully extended with his arms just as contact was made. Players would bounce off his hands, and it looked like he was exerting almost no force to them.

My all-time best punch came against Al "Bubba" Baker, who played for the St. Louis Cardinals and Cleveland Browns. He was coming in to me from the outside and was trying a move where he would grab the cloth on the back of my shoulder pads, pull back with his upper body, trying to pull me forward, and then use a swim move to get around me. He tried for the grab but missed. His body was just starting to pull back when I made contact with his chest. I literally lifted his feet off the ground with my punch and he ended up on his butt, looking up at me. We were both stunned by what happened. He said that was the best pass block that anyone had ever done on him. (But that didn't slow him down for the rest of the game, or the other times I played him.)

A good pass protector is also very calm. There can be mass insanity going on around you, but you must block it all out and calmly react to the rusher. When you get in the groove, it is like a hitter in baseball who can see the seams on the baseball as it comes in, reading what type of pitch it is. The ball looks as big as a beach ball and as easy to hit. With practice, you will see the various

Some guys will get a clock in their head and start to panic once they think the passer should have gotten the ball off. We used to kid Phil Simms that he held on to the ball forever, testing our abilities to keep the rushers at bay. During meetings, when he did this, we would all start humming the "Final Jeopardy" theme, letting him know that he didn't have thirty seconds to make up his mind. The offensive lineman's job is not done, however, until the quarterback has gotten rid of the ball, no matter how long it takes.

While helping to coach the Giants in 1989 while I was recovering from the chemotherapy required to heal my Hodgkin's disease, I was assigned to help a rookie by the name of Eric Moore. He was playing both guard and tackle, and was getting his butt beaten by pass rushers even worse than I had been. I tried everything I could think of talking to him about technique: keeping his head and shoulders back, thumbs up, back straight, and hips down. He kept burying his head in the defender's chest, worse than I ever did. He didn't have a chance to make the squad if he kept this up. Finally I told him to do what my old coach, Tom Bresnahan, told me to do. I said I didn't care if he hit anyone, just keep his head back. I would talk to the coaches for him if it didn't work. He tried it for a series, came back to me and said, "Gee, that really works." I could have killed him. I had been telling him about the techniques for over two weeks, but he just refused to try them. When he did, he started to have some real success. I guess that was payback for all the headaches I had caused my coaches in the past.

pass rush techniques being used by the rusher and can calmly react to them. Anthony Munoz, the Hall of Fame left tackle for the Cincinnati Bengals, was an expert at this. He took every set the same and calmly blocked his man until the ball was away. I loved to watch film of him; he was so smooth and calm.

I had very little instruction on proper pass protection techniques in high school and college. Both places were only concerned with results. They didn't care how you got it done, as long as you did it. I was a good enough athlete that I got it done despite technique that was less than perfect.

That ended quickly when I got to the Giants training camp in 1983, my rookie year. I kept lunging toward the pass rusher, putting my head down, and I kept getting beaten. My balance was so bad and the rushers were so good that I looked terrible. I was wondering if I belonged at this level. My coach, Tom Bresnahan, kept telling me to keep my head and shoulders back, but I panicked when the rusher got close, wanting to get my hands on him and deliver a blow to slow him down. Finally, after about a week of getting beaten, my coach pulled me aside and said he didn't care if I hit a single person in pass rush drills that day. He just wanted me to keep my head and shoulders back and see what happened. I was terrified, but I did as I was told, and I had much better success. I still got beaten occasionally, but not because of having my weight forward and being off-balance.

Pass Protection

Pass protection is slightly different for each of the positions of the offensive line. Much of this is based upon where the quarterback is setting up. If a lineman does not know the point he is trying to protect, how can he protect it?

Let's start with the standard straight back drop by the quarterback. The two classic drops are a five-step drop and a seven-step drop. In the pros, a five-step drop gets the quarterback about six to seven yards deep, while a seven-step drop will get him about nine yards deep. With younger players, these drops are usually at five and seven yards respectively. The quarterback will set up directly behind the center. The quarterback will need to be able to step up in the pocket to throw, so the area that needs to be protected is a circle of about two yards in radius around the drop point.

The key to positioning for pass protection is not to get beaten to the inside, especially for the tackles. An offensive lineman always wants to take away the most direct path to the quarterback. This is most important for the tackles. If a tackle gets beaten to the inside, the defender has to take two or three fewer steps to get to the quarterback than if he beats the tackle to the outside. There is less of a difference for the guard, and no difference for the center, since the quarterback is setting up directly behind him. Also, you want to keep the middle clear so the quarterback has a place where he can step up if he feels pressure from the outside. Knowing this, the lineman can "cheat" a little on his positioning, favoring the inside and forcing the defender to go outside.

The easiest way to visualize this is to form a cup or semicircle in front of where the quarterback is going to set up. Once you get to the depth of the quarterback, the circle flattens out because you do not have to run the rusher three yards behind the quarterback. When pass protection is done to perfection, you will see a semicircle about four to seven yards in diameter, with a blocker directly between the rusher and the quarterback (see fig. 9.1).

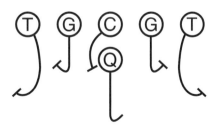

Figure 9.1 Cup pass protection

The offensive lineman will want to keep himself between the defender and the quarterback at all times. The lineman should also know where he has help or where he has more of a margin of error. For example, the three interior linemen, the center and two guards, will generally be responsible for two down linemen, so unless there is a blitz, at least one of them will have some help from an adjacent lineman. Tackles are usually in a one-on-one situation, with no help to either side.

The Center

The center has probably the hardest job of all the linemen initially because he not only has to block, but he must first get the ball back to the quarterback. While snapping the ball, he should drive his off hand up as fast as possible into the rusher's chest. Once the exchange is made, the other hand should follow. The defender knows that the center will be delayed in getting his snap hand up and will often attack that side of the center first. Knowing this, the center's first step should be a small lateral step to the side of his snap hand, giving him a little help in fending off this first move. This will move him slightly off-center of the defender until he gets his snap hand up. Once that hand gets up, he should move to be directly in front of the rusher.

If the rusher is initially offset to one side or the other, the initial step should bring the center to the position where he can protect his snap hand until he gets it up. For example, if the rusher is lined up over his off hand, he should step with that foot and slide over, but not go all the way to the middle of the defender because the snap hand should be slightly protected. Once both hands are up, they should be on the rusher's chest, arms fully extended, thumbs up, elbows close together with the bend pointing down, with one hand at the top of each number. The center's feet and hips should be parallel to the line of scrimmage. As the rusher moves to one side or the other, the center can be slightly off-center to him, favoring the inside, since that is where you do not want to get beaten. If the center knows he has help to one side or the other, he can also be slightly off-center to the side away from where the help is. If the rusher feels he is being overplayed, he will go the other way, right into the help. The center should give ground grudgingly, trying to force the rusher to go wide to whichever side the rusher wants to work. As the rusher gets wider, he can then let him start to come upfield. Remember the cup that you want to keep around the quarterback; the wider you run the defender, the more you can allow him to come upfield.

The Guard

The guard has the easiest job of the offensive line positions, in theory. He doesn't have to snap the ball, and he has someone on each side of him to limit how wide a rusher can go to try to beat him. However he also has the most potential types of twists (linemen and/or backers crossing) to deal with, so it is not that easy. We will talk more about that later.

In a straight drop back pass situation, the quarterback will set up directly behind the center. Because the guard does not want to get beaten inside, he should slightly favor this direction when pass protecting. He should try to be a little more dominant with the inside hand than with the outside hand. The inside hand should still aim for the inside number, while the outside hand aims for the outside number, but more pressure should be applied with the inside hand. The guard can have his outside foot slightly farther back than his inside foot, but not by more than a couple of inches. The hips should stay square to the line of scrimmage. The shoulders should initially be square to the line of scrimmage. Of course, the head and shoulders are back, the arms straight, and the thumbs up.

If the rusher takes an inside move, the guard should step hard with his inside foot, trying to flatten him out down the line of scrimmage and not give ground. You must try to keep the integrity of the pocket or cup around the quarterback. If the guard allows the rusher to gain ground while taking an inside move, this will break down the cup. If the rusher takes an outside move, the guard can try to slide him to the outside. If he gives some ground in this technique, that is fine. The wider the guard takes the rusher, the more ground he can give.

The Tackle

After the ball is snapped, the tackle has the toughest job of the linemen. He is generally blocking one-on-one and is usually going against the best pass rushers. The two positions that Coach Parcells rode hardest in practice were cornerbacks and offensive tackles. If a cornerback gets beaten, you give up seven points. If a tackle gets beaten, you can lose your quarterback.

Because the quarterback is setting up behind the center and the tackle is farthest from the center, the tackle should favor the inside the most of any lineman. If the rusher starts out head up, the first move has to be a slide step inward with the inside foot. After this slide step, the tackle's head should be centered on the inside edge of the rusher's inside number. While taking the slide step, the inside hand should shoot out and hit the rusher just within the inside armpit. Try to get full extension with this arm. The other hand should come up as quickly as possible and get onto the rusher's outside number. The shoulders and hips should stay parallel to the line of scrimmage, but the outside foot should be back about four to six inches. The tackle wants to encourage the rusher to take an upfield rush, which is why he sets so far inside. If the rusher takes an inside move, you want to flatten him out down the line of scrimmage and keep him moving parallel to the line of scrimmage, and not up into the pocket. If the rusher goes to the outside, try to widen him a little, but don't put so much outside pressure as to encourage an inside move. Straight upfield force is fine.

If the rusher is lined slightly off-center to the outside of the offensive tackle, the tackle should just lift and replace his inside foot at the snap while bringing his inside hand up into the rusher. You never want to start a play with your feet planted, so some type of foot movement is necessary. Your feet and body are already in perfect position to take on the rusher, slightly to the inside with your outside foot about six inches farther back than the inside. This sounds like the easiest situation, but it can actually be difficult. The tendency is to step forward with your inside foot, since you want to move a foot at the snap to get the rest of the body going. This is not good because it reduces the distance between you and the rusher when you don't have to, and it is always to your advantage to keep that space.

If the rusher is on the outside shoulder or wider, the first step should be taken with the outside foot. The problem most tackles have in this situation is that they false step forward with their outside foot so they can push back harder out of their stance. It is a false step because it is a step that is not helping you get back off the ball. When this step is taken, it allows the rusher to get one step farther upfield, making it harder to block him.

The distance of the outward step is determined by how far outside the rusher is. The wider he is, the farther the outside foot needs to go back. If the rusher is just on the outside shoulder, then the foot can go just slightly outside and

I played against Mark Gastineau in my rookie season of 1984. Gastineau set the sack record that year with twenty-one sacks, no thanks to me. I shut him out that game. (I tell Michael Strahan, the Giants defensive end who now holds the record, that he owes me one.) I thought I had a great game. I was even interviewed by John Madden and Pat Summerall after the game, the first time they ever interviewed an offensive lineman on air after the game. The only thing Gastineau said to me all day was, "You are a hardworking son of a bitch." I don't think that anyone has ever paid me a nicer compliment.

Someone forgot to tell my offensive line coach, Tom Bresnahan, what a great game I had. That following Monday when we watched the film of the game, he kept yelling at me because my first step when Gastineau was outside was at a 30-degree angle rather than the 60-degree angle it should have been. On that day, I was a good enough athlete and sometimes lucky enough to get away with the incorrect step. He was right, of course, so I went out to practice that week and concentrated on that first step.

back at a 45-degree angle. If the rusher is a yard or more outside, then the step should be taken at a 60-degree angle, gaining as much depth as possible.

As the rusher moves upfield, the tackle will have a tendency to turn his body to stay face-to-face with the rusher. While his head and shoulders do need to turn, the hips should stay parallel to the line of scrimmage and the toes should stay pointing toward the line. The tackle's outside foot should be farther and farther back as his distance from the line of scrimmage increases. At about six yards deep you want the outside foot to be at a 60-degree angle to the line of scrimmage, but with the hips and toes forward. This may sound crazy, but it will leave you in a much better position to counter the moves the rusher may attempt.

If the tackle allows the rusher to come upfield six yards, and then the rusher takes an inside move, just pushing him parallel to the line of scrimmage will not be good enough. You will run him right into the step-up and follow-through area for the quarterback. This will either flush the quarterback out of the pocket or, if he is throwing the ball, the follow-through of his arm will go into the rusher, risking injury. If the rusher goes inside after he has gone this far upfield, the tackle must work to drive him back toward the line of scrimmage as he takes him inside. This is where having the hips and toes facing forward comes into play.

When we talked about drive blocking, we said that the power comes from the toes pointing forward. This will direct the power. You can use the full power of the legs, hips, and low back only if you are using them in a forward motion. When you need to get forward movement on the man going inside, you can have much more strength if your feet are already lined up in that direction.

Another benefit of having the hips and toes forward is that it will firm up the outside shoulder of the tackle. With the hips forward, the upper body is already turned 30 to 45 degrees to the outside. The upper body can turn only so far before the muscles in the side will not allow it to turn any more. At 45 degrees you are close to this point. If the rusher then attacks the outside shoulder, it can't move back very far before the body naturally stops further rotation, giving the rusher a hard corner to go around. If the hips are facing the rusher and he attacks the outside shoulder, that shoulder can be pushed back 45 degrees before it comes to that support point. This causes a soft corner for the rusher to push through, making it much easier for the rusher to beat the tackle to the outside. So by having the hips and toes forward, it gives you an advantage whether the rusher is trying to go inside or to beat the outside shoulder.

The farther the rusher comes upfield, the more likely he is to stop and try to come underneath for an inside move. Because of this, the farther upfield the tackle is with the rusher, the more predominant the inside hand should be. When you get to the depth of the quarterback, only the inside hand should be on the rusher. At this time, to keep his momentum going upfield, you can turn your feet and hips toward the man and, using the inside arm, continue to drive him upfield. In photo 9.3 on the next page, I have run the defender to the level of the quarterback, have turned my hips to the outside, and have lowered my inside hand to his ribcage in order to make him run past the quarterback and stop any inside move he may try.

The wider the rusher is before the snap, the farther back from the line of scrimmage the first contact will occur. The tackle should drop at a 60-degree angle to the line, the same as his first step. If the tackle goes too flat along the line, his momentum will be too much to the outside and will make him susceptible to a hard inside move. It also does not give as good an angle if the rusher "speed rushes" upfield. If he goes straight back at a 90-degree angle, the first contact will be too close to the quarterback and leave very little room for mistakes.

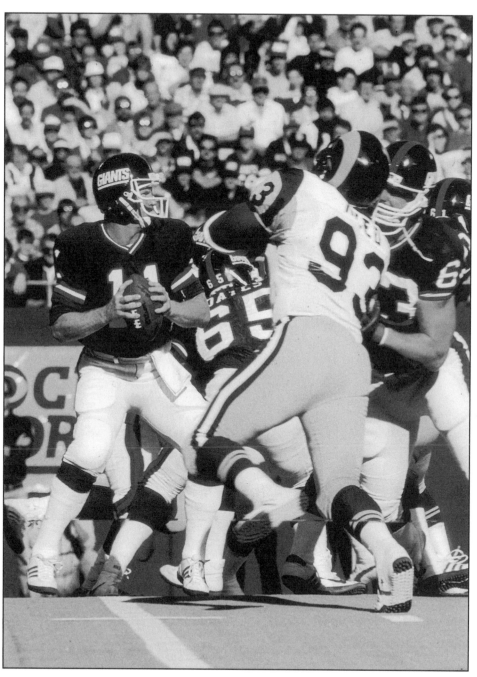

Photo 9.3 Protecting the passer

Credit: Jerry Pinkus

10

Defending Pass Rush Techniques

We have discussed techniques for pass protection, but that is just the start. A pass rusher is not just going to come into you and give up his chest so you can get good position with your inside hand and control him as described in the previous chapter. Pass rushers will use a number of basic moves and techniques to defeat the block and get a sack. Knowing what these are and how to counter them will make you a better pass protector.

Defeating the Bull Rush

The bull rush is where the rusher tries to run over you. He will come out of his stance low and hard, trying to get his hands inside yours and his head below yours. Since you are in a more upright position to pass protect, keeping your head back for balance, he may initially be able to get under you. Work to get your hands on the inside for control, and drop your hips and butt to lower your center of gravity. Widen your base for more balance and power. Get your weight on your toes so you can push forward more easily, but try not to lower your head forward into the rusher—this is what he wants. If you lean forward too much, he will stop, pull you forward and out of the way, and go around you.

This is a tricky area to teach because you must give resistance without getting too much weight forward. It is a very fine line and will take much practice to get the proper feel. If you are still getting pushed back, grab the bottom of the rusher's shoulder pads at the chest and lift them upward. This will take the force that he is applying in a straight-ahead motion and move that momentum upward where it will not work against you. This is simple physics. If a force is being applied straight forward at a unit value of 100, then the full force is felt straight ahead. If that force can be redirected so it is going up at a 45-degree angle, then only about 70 units of force are actually being directed forward, making the rusher easier to stop.

Defeating the Slap or Club

The most basic pass rush move is the slap or club, where the rusher comes in and slaps the blocker's shoulder hard with a sideways blow, causing the blocker to go off-balance and allowing the rusher a seam to rush the quarterback. This move is especially effective when an outside rusher gets a tackle moving upfield and then slaps the inside shoulder. Because the tackle's momentum is already going upfield, it is easier to get movement and come underneath. That is why balance is the key to pass protecting. Even though you are moving in one direction (backward and to the outside in this case), you must be prepared to go the opposite direction immediately.

The easiest way to counter the slap when you see it coming is to stab the rusher in the chest with your arm that is to the side the slap is coming from. It is like a boxing trainer with pads on his hands who flashes the pads toward the boxer for the boxer to hit. Here, instead of hitting the "pad" when you see it coming, you will strike out and hit the rusher in the chest. You can tell when a slap is coming because, to get any power on it, the rusher will have to drop his arm down before he swings it up to hit you. When you see this, stab out. His chest will be unprotected and easy to hit if you are quick enough.

The double slap is exactly as it sounds. The rusher will slap with one hand and then immediately counter with a slap with the other, hoping that you put too much effort into stopping the first slap. Good balance will prevent this from working. He can slap all day, just sit in there with good balance and keep countering—stabbing into the armpit as you see each blow coming.

Defeating the Swim Move

Many rushers will follow the slap with an arm over or swim move. The rusher tries to get past you by slapping a shoulder and then attacking that shoulder by raising up the opposite arm and using a low overhead freestyle-type swimming stroke, working to get the swimming arm over and behind you to "swim" past. If the arm gets past you he will hook you with it and pull himself past you and on to the quarterback. This technique works best for the rusher if you are dropping your head forward and allowing him to get into your body. The initial slap is to try to push you to the side and get you off-balance. The easiest way to stop the swim or arm over is to stab with your hand into the rusher's chest on the side of his initial slap. This will take all the power away from him on the slap and will also keep him far away.

When he tries the arm over, stab the hand on the side of the arm going over into that armpit and drive him to the side with this hand. The problem with this move is that it exposes the rusher's chest and side. If you keep your head back and keep him away from you, this is a very easy move to combat. If you have your head down and allow the rusher into your body, it is a very effective move. George Martin, whom I practiced against every day with the Giants, had the best swim move I ever saw.

Defeating the Rip

The arm rip is also an effective move. The person who did this move the best I ever saw or played against was Howie Long of the Raiders. The arm rip, as most moves, starts with a slap to the shoulder to try to get you off-balance. The rusher's next move is to take his opposite arm and throw it hard or "rip" it between the blocker's arm and body, trying to get the shoulder all the way into the blocker's armpit. He will then continue to raise up the rip arm, lifting the blocker's arm, until he can go under the arm and in for the sack. To counter this move, as always, keep the head back and keep the rusher at arm's length. If his rip gets into your armpit, clamp down on his rip arm with your arm that he is trying to go under, pinning it against your side. Swing your hips in front of him and take your off hand and push on his hip to push him wide.

When Howie started using this move he was almost impossible to stop because if you tried to pin his arm with yours, the refs would call holding on the blocker. This move was so good that the league had to do something to help out offensive linemen, so they legalized the pinning of the rip arm. If he is going to stick it in there, the blocker should be able to do something with it.

Defeating the Hand Slap

The hand slap technique is effective for the rusher if the blocker keeps his hands out too far in front or if he has too much weight forward when taking on the rusher. The move is just as it sounds. As the rusher comes in and the blocker puts his hands out to stab, the rusher slaps down with his hands on those of the blocker. If the blocker is leaning forward too much, anticipating the contact with the rusher and the resistance from the contact, and then gets no contact or resistance, he will be off-balance forward and in no position to pass protect. The defender may just run around the off-balance blocker or use a combination hand slap/swim or hand slap/rip. To counter the hand slap, if you can read it quickly enough, simply pull your hands back before the rusher can hit them. Even if he slaps your hands down, if your head is back and you are not leaning too far forward, he will just be able to get a bit closer to you than you would optimally want. If he gets close, drop your butt lower, bring your arms back up and get your hands inside his, then get extension with your arms back to where you want to be.

Defeating the Spin Move

The spin move is used by the rusher when he thinks you are overplaying one direction or if he thinks you are off-balance to one side. This move is best executed when the rusher is close to your body. When he comes out of his spin move he will want to catch you with his elbow and use it as a hook to finish

Some players develop their own special type of move based on the physical attributes they have. In my rookie season I played against Jack Youngblood of the L.A. Rams. It was his fifteenth season and my first. It was the worst game of my entire career. He had incredibly strong hands. When I went to stab my hands out to stop him, he would grab the back of my outside arm with his hand. If I was in bad position, which happened often that day, he would just pull himself around me and go in and hit Phil Simms, our quarterback. If I was in good position, he would pull me down on top of him and there was a ref on the sideline that would call *me* for holding. I ended up with three holding calls in the game. Parcells wanted to kill me, and I didn't want to come to our sideline after a couple of our series.

   We had to play the Rams again in the wildcard playoff game that year. I had to block Youngblood again. I watched film on how to block him. I asked other players what I should do. They said just do the basics, head back and arms out. I had done this the first time and got killed. How was I going to stop him from grabbing my arm? We flew out to L.A. and I still had no idea what I was going to do differently. I got to the stadium about four hours early, as I usually did—still without a game plan. I was sitting across from the training room when it hit me. Vaseline. Before our first series I had the trainer put Vaseline on the back of my right arm. The first pass play Jack came in and grabbed my arm. I was in good position so he tried to pull me down. His hand slid off and he ended up falling down. I had big red scratch marks on the back of my arm. He couldn't say anything to the refs because the front of his jersey was so slick from spraying silicone on it that I could barely keep contact with him. Sometimes you have to do whatever it takes to get the job done.

pulling himself around you. For example, let's assume that the rusher is coming upfield on your outside shoulder, doing a hand slap toward the outside to get in close to your body, then spinning to the inside. The best way to defeat a spin is to simply keep the man away from you. If he is at arm's length and spins, he will just do a pirouette and not get anywhere. If he gets body-to-body

Photo 10.1 Countering the spin move

and you feel the spin coming, push him in the back with the hand toward the direction he is spinning to knock him off-balance while sliding your feet and body in that direction also (see photo 10.1). Not an easy thing to do, but if you don't let him into your body, the move will never work.

Defeating Combination Moves

Then there are combination moves where the rusher will combine two or more moves in succession to beat the blocker. Basically the first move will be to either get the blocker off-balance or get the rusher into the blocker's body. For example, the rusher will combine the hand slap with a swim move, since the swim is easier to do from close in. Or he can do a rip spin, where he comes in like he is going to use the rip move to get the blocker leaning that way, then follows with a spin to the other side. If proper technique is used, the rusher can try any number of moves, but as long as they are countered properly, he will be flailing away many yards from the quarterback and of no danger. Most rushers will try one or two moves, then go to a bull rush when those do not work.

Keeping the Passing Lanes Open

The last move a rusher will try is to get his hands up in the passing lanes to try to bat down the ball being thrown. If he jumps to do this, the easiest and most effective counter is to punch out and hit the rusher in the stomach or lower. This will encourage him not to jump in the future. If he just puts his hands up, then he is giving you his chest and he is also stopping his forward momentum, so you should get aggressive and drive into him, pushing him back and trying to get a pancake block on him, putting him flat on his back. If you get him down like this, he will be too embarrassed to try to put his hands up in the future.

> I know what it is like to get a ball batted like this. When the Giants played the Dallas Cowboys, I had to block Ed "Too Tall" Jones, who was 6'9". Late in a close game we were throwing the ball on third down. I had Too Tall wired just off the line of scrimmage, about five yards away from Phil Simms, our quarterback. Brad Benson, our left tackle, had run his man, Jimmy Jeffcoat, about three yards behind Phil, well out of the play. Phil threw the ball, Too Tall batted it straight back, and it fell into the hands of Jeffcoat, who grabbed it and ran about fifty yards for a touchdown. We ended up losing the game because of this play—even though both Brad and I did our jobs, the result was negative.

Defeating Stunts

Rushers will also work together to help each other beat the blockers. They will run two- or three-man games or twists. When naming twists, we generally named them based on who was going first on the twist. For example, an "E-T," or end-tackle twist, is when the defensive end goes inside and the defensive tackle circles behind him. A "T-E," or tackle-end twist, would be just the opposite.

Let's look at the E-T first. The defensive end will come upfield a couple of steps and then take a hard inside move. While he is doing this, the defensive tackle will engage the guard, trying to keep him close to the line of scrimmage. When the defensive end makes his inside move, he will try to hit the guard on his side and push him to the inside (see fig. 10.1). The defensive tackle will circle behind the end and take the outside rush lane. If done properly, the guard is knocked off the defensive tackle and cannot get back to block the defensive end. This leaves two people for the offensive tackle to block.

There are two ways to take on a twist: by switching men, which is the most common and usually easiest method, and by staying man-to-man and fighting through the twist. The San Francisco 49ers back in the 1980s were one of the few pro teams I have seen who consistently manned twists.

To defend the E-T by switching, when the defensive end takes his hard inside move, the tackle has to push the defensive end toward the line of scrimmage so that he cannot pick the guard. The tackle knows that he can never get beaten inside—and should be driving the end flat anyway. The guard needs to read the twist as soon as he can. He should be able to tell that the defensive tackle is not putting a full rush on him. When he reads this he should yell "twist" and look in the direction the twist is coming from. As the defensive end comes down on the guard, the guard should take his hand to that side and get it in front of the defensive end, accepting the block from the tackle. The tackle needs to stay on the defensive end until he is sure that the guard has him. It will take some time for the defensive tackle to get around to the outside and be in a position to threaten the quarterback. You always want to have the inside man blocked first because he has the most direct path to the quarterback.

Manning an E-T twist is dangerous because there is nothing to stop the defensive end from coming down to pick the guard. When manning, the tackle will take a deep set and read what the defensive end does. If he goes inside, the tackle will be too far back to come up and stop him from picking the guard. The guard will have to read the pick and either push his man forward to avoid the pick or take on the defensive end and fight behind him to then pick up the

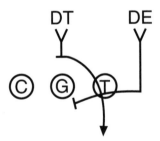

Figure 10.1 End-tackle twist

defensive tackle. The main reason that you man a twist is because if the rusher going first grabs and holds the man initially blocking him and then picks the blocker next to him, it allows his teammate to come clean. By deep setting, the tackle does not allow the defensive end to grab him and still be able to pick the guard. By the way, grabbing like this by the defense is illegal, but that doesn't mean it will be called.

Stopping the T-E twist by switching is similar to stopping the E-T. The defensive tackle will attack the guard's outside, trying to get between the guard and tackle. The defensive end will initially come right at the tackle, trying to keep him close to the line of scrimmage (see fig. 10.2). The defensive tackle will then either pick the tackle or try to get to the side and behind the tackle so the tackle cannot block him. The defensive end will circle around the defensive tackle, leaving two men for the guard to block. To stop the T-E, the guard must make sure that he keeps the defensive tackle flat and not allow him to get penetration to the side of or behind the tackle. The tackle, when he reads the twist, should first yell "twist," then come inside hard to take on the defensive tackle, making sure he gets his inside arm in front of the defensive tackle. It should be a lateral step, keeping the shoulders facing the line of scrimmage. The guard, once he feels the tackle take over the defensive tackle, will then have time to pick up the looping defensive end, who will be coming to his inside.

Stopping the T-E by manning the twist is easy. The guard will just ride the defensive tackle to the outside and deep, and the tackle, since he is deep setting, will have plenty of time and space to loop behind the guard and pick up the twisting defensive end. Manning is very effective against the T-E if the first

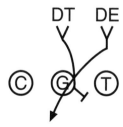

Figure 10.2 Tackle-end twist

rusher is grabbing. If he is not grabbing, zone is just as easy, and to be consistent, zone should always be used unless the defender is grabbing.

Twists between men over the guards and/or the center are handled in the same way. The blocker with the man going first must keep his man as flat to the line of scrimmage as possible, while the blocker with the rusher going behind must read it and attack the first man on the twist. If there is ever a problem, always block the first man and let the man going behind go free because it will take him longer to get to the quarterback. The first blocker must never leave the first rusher until he knows his teammate has control of the man he is passing off. Once again, the first man can cause problems more quickly, so you are better off double-teaming him rather than passing him off to no one.

You will occasionally see three-man games or twists where the front-side defensive end and defensive tackle slant inside and the weak-side defensive tackle comes around both of them to the outside on the strong side. With the Giants, we called this a "Yipsi" because our offensive line coach had a coach that first saw the move at a small college called Ypsilanti. The move takes forever to run, and seldom have I seen it have success, but you should be prepared for it.

To defend the "yipsi" is no different than any other twist, except the middle man will have to do a double pass-off (see fig. 10.3). The middle blocker (guard) takes the middle rusher flat to the man next to him (tackle). Since the tackle's man is the one running around two other people, he will take off very quickly, allowing the tackle to come down and take over the middle rusher. A twist should be called as soon as it is recognized. Instead of then picking up the rusher coming around the first man, the middle blocker (guard) will have to

The Washington Redskins were very good at running twists, especially T-Es. Dave Butts, the defensive tackle, was huge and was very good at grabbing the guards. Charles Mann, the defensive end, was very fast and could get around the corner quickly. One year, to cross up the Redskins, when we broke the huddle I would call to my guard, Chris Godfrey, either "man" or "zone." If we guessed right and it was a T-E, this made the block easy. We knew their tendencies and were able to greatly frustrate the Redskins. They ended up not running as many twists because of this, and that made our jobs easier.

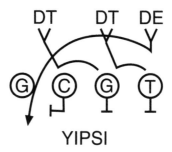

Figure 10.3 Yipsi stunt

come back and take over the rusher from the man on the other side of him (center). He must stay on his man a long time, even if he sees the loop man start to come around. The inside man always has priority. The second pass-off will be made, and the looping rusher will be picked up by the blocker (center) who passed off the second rusher. Sounds confusing, but if you communicate the twists between players, this will help greatly.

11

Blitz Pickup

In order to discuss blitz pickups, first we must define what a blitz is. Many teams call it a blitz anytime more than four people rush the quarterback. If you are facing a four down linemen defense, anytime a backer rushes it will be considered a blitz. If you are facing a three down lineman front, one backer may rush and most teams would not consider it a blitz. It would take two additional rushers to make it a blitz.

We will look at two main defenses. The first is a 4-3 or a 6-1, which covers the two guards and two tackles with backers over the tight ends and also lined up behind the line over the center. It will also be called an even front because there is an even number of down linemen (see fig. 11.1 on the next page). The other defense is a 3-4 with a nose man over the center, defensive ends over the offensive tackles, backers over the tight ends, and backers off the line over the guards (see fig. 11.2 on the next page). This is called an odd defense. You may also see an additional rover back somewhere off the line of scrimmage if the defense is playing an eight-man front.

The old basic blitz pickup that I grew up with had the covered linemen responsible for the down linemen over them and the uncovered linemen responsible for a backer who was lined up over them. The backs or tight ends were responsible for the outside backers. If the outside backers didn't come, the backs

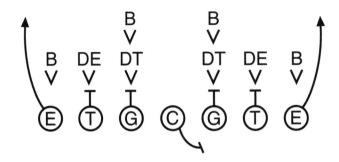

Figure 11.1 Base protection against an even defense

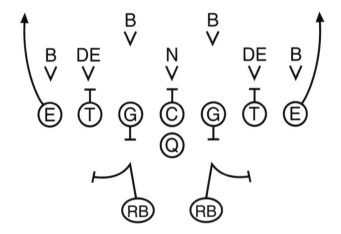

Figure 11.2 Base protection against an odd defense

would release into their pass routes. If the inside backers didn't come, the uncovered linemen would help to either side, depending on where help was needed.

Slide Protection

In the base blitz pickup everything is *base blocked*, or blocked with a basic rule that covers most situations. Covered big men block the men over them. ("Big on big.") Uncovered big men block the backer off the line closest to them. Outside

An old teammate of mine changed my notion of the blitz. The man who changed blitz pickups was Lawrence Taylor. He redefined the position of outside line-backer. Before he came into the league the typical outside backer was 6'2", 220 pounds, and on passing plays was responsible for dropping into coverage. If he did rush, the back was usually good enough to pick him up. Most of the good pass rushing backers were the inside backers.

L.T. was 6'4" and 245 pounds with incredible athletic ability and strength. Teams that tried to block him with a back quickly found out that if they wanted to keep their quarterback on his feet, this was not a good idea. L.T. actually became such a great rusher by mistake and mental errors. At the snap of the ball, he would sometimes forget, or purposely not remember, whether he was supposed to drop into coverage or to rush the passer. Every time he wasn't sure he would just rush the passer, usually with great success. He often got to the quarterback before the quarterback could find the man he was supposed to be covering. After a while the coaches figured that since L.T. was just going to rush the passer anyway, they would devise defenses to allow him to do this.

Since a back couldn't block him, the offense had to find a way to get a line-man on him. Because the Giants played a 3-4 or odd defense, the guard to the side of L.T. was given the honor of doing what is called scan protection. At the snap, he would drop back while looking at the inside backer to his side. If that inside backer did not come, then he would go behind the tackle to pick up the outside backer, namely L.T. The problem with this was that L.T. now had a run-ning start at the guard, and with his strength he was able to run over the guard or at least push him back into the quarterback. The next option was to fan block, where the guard would fan out to the defensive end over the tackle and the tackle would fan out to the outside backer to his outside. This was better because you were getting a big body on L.T. quickly, but he was still able to run over people as big as Joe Jacoby who was 6'8" and 320 pounds. He was a giant in the mid-'80s.

Hopefully no one reading this book will have to block L.T. This is merely an example of how you may have to improvise to block certain people or unusual defenses.

backers are picked up by the backs. The problem with this is that if the opponent brings the outside backers, the backs, your quickest players and best ball carriers, can never get out into a pattern. To solve this you slide the protection to the side of the back that you want to get out into the pattern. If you are sliding to the left, the covered linemen on the right side of the line block the men over them.

The slide starts at the first uncovered lineman (see fig. 11.3). For an even defense, the front-side guard and tackle block the men over them. The back staying in will check the right inside backer. If he doesn't come, the back will then check for the outside backer on the right. If neither comes he can either help a lineman or release into a route. The uncovered center turns back toward the left guard, with his first step being a step back with his left foot. If the defensive tackle over the guard comes to his face, he will take him. If the defensive tackle goes to the outside, there will probably be a backer coming to his face on a blitz. The left guard will turn back toward the tackle, stepping back with his outside foot.

It is important that the guard stab out with his inside (right) arm toward the defensive tackle who lined up over him. If the defensive tackle goes to the outside and to the face of the guard, the guard must take him. If he does not stab out with that inside arm, the defensive tackle will hit him in the side, leaving him for the center. By stabbing out, the guard will automatically engage the tackle

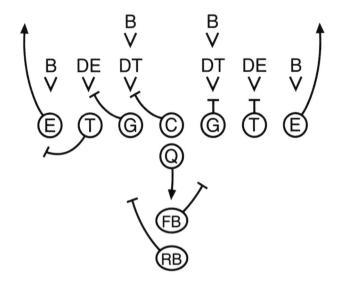

Figure 11.3 Slide protection against an even defense

if he makes an outside move. But if a backer is blitzing to the center-guard gap, that will leave the center to block two people. The left tackle will set back, stepping with his outside foot first at a 60-degree angle just like he was only blocking the backer outside of him. He also needs to stab out with his inside arm toward the defensive end over him in case the defensive end is taking an outside move and comes to his face. If the defensive end is taking an outside move, either the backer is dropping off into coverage, or the backer and defensive end are running a twist with the backer going behind the defensive end.

With an odd defense, the right tackle has the defensive end over him one-on-one. The back staying in checks the front-side inside backer. If he is not coming, he then looks for the outside backer to his side. The slide starts with the right guard. He will turn toward the center, dropping his left foot back. If the nose tackle comes to his face, he will take him. If the nose works away, he should look for a blitzer in the gap. The center turns to his left, dropping his left foot. He needs to stab out with his right arm toward the nose tackle so that he can take him over if the nose comes to his face. If the nose does not come to his face, he should look for a blitzing backer (see fig. 11.4). The slide continues down the line as described previously. If linemen are covered, they need to stab out with their right arm as they turn at the man over them. If they are uncovered, they turn to take the man over the lineman next to them.

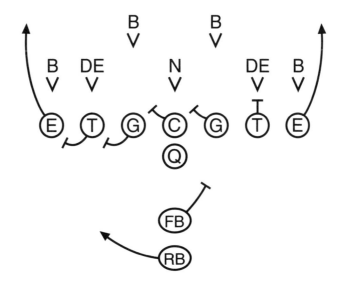

Figure 11.4 Slide protection against an odd defense

Scan Protection

Scan protection is used if you want to try to get both backs out into patterns. The basic concept of scan protection is that uncovered linemen can be responsible for at least two people. If the first one comes, then either a back or the quarterback has to read the second potential blitzer and if he is coming react accordingly.

First, let's look at the odd front (see fig. 11.5). In this set, both guards are uncovered. Their job is to read the backers over them first, and if the backers do not come on a blitz, then the guards will drop back and out, looking for the outside backer on their side to blitz. The first step should be back with the outside foot to get moving back and to the side in case the outside backer comes. If the inside backer comes, the guard will still have plenty of time to react to him even though he is initially going back and to the outside. If the backer he is responsible for goes to the inside and runs a twist behind the nose man, the guard needs to be able to get the depth to get behind the center and pick up the blitz. If the inside man does not come, then the guard has to work out to a point outside of the offensive tackle if the outside backer is blitzing to the outside. If neither man comes, then he can go back to the inside and help out either the tackle or center. The idea of scan protection is to get the back out, but the

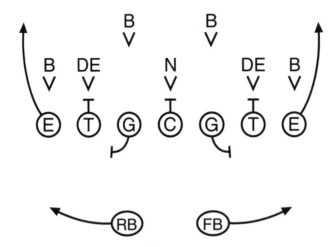

Figure 11.5 Scan protection against an odd defense

back may have responsibilities before he can release. He needs to check the inside backer to his side first. If he is not coming, then he has a free release. If the inside backer to his side is coming, then he needs to check the outside backer to his side. If he comes, then the back must pick him up unless there is a hot read on the play. A hot read means that the quarterback knows that there is a man coming in unblocked and he needs to dump the ball off to a hot receiver quickly. Since both the backers to one side are coming, there should be no one who can quickly get to the back on that side and he is the hot dump.

With an eight-man front, it is harder to get both backs out on a pass (see fig. 11.6). You can scan to either side. If you want to get the back out on the right, you would have the uncovered lineman, the center, scan to the right. On the snap, he would drop back while looking at the right inside backer. If he comes, the center will pick him up. If he does not, then the center will scan out to the right outside backer. If he doesn't come, then he will help either the right guard or right tackle. If the right inside backer comes on a blitz, then the back who is trying to release to the outside has to look for the right outside backer and pick him up if he is blitzing or keep releasing and be the hot receiver on the play.

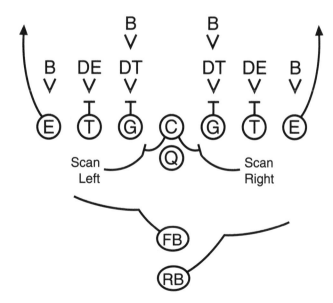

Figure 11.6 Scan protection against an even defense

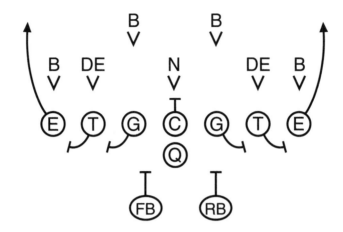

Figure 11.7 Fan protection to both sides against an odd defense

Fan Protection

Fan protection is used when you do not expect many blitzes from the inside backers and the backs cannot be expected to block the outside backers either because of size or because of the pass rushing skills of the backers. For an odd front, fan protection is exactly like slide protection, except the blocking scheme is done by only the guard and tackle working to the outside for the defensive end and outside linebacker (see fig. 11.7). The footwork is the same as described for slide protection. For an even front, fan and slide protection are exactly the same (see fig. 11.8).

Max Protection

Max, or maximum, protection is exactly what it sounds like. Everyone is responsible for the man over him, keeping the backs and tight ends in to block. The only people out on the route are the wide receivers. This is used when you are expecting a full blitz and you know that your receiver can beat the coverage. For an odd front, the front seven block the men over them and the backs are there to help out or to pick up defensive backs that might be blitzing (see fig. 11.9). With an even front, which way the center goes will be determined by the direc-

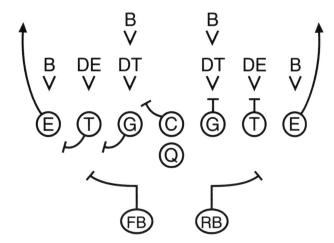

Figure 11.8 Fan left protection against an even defense

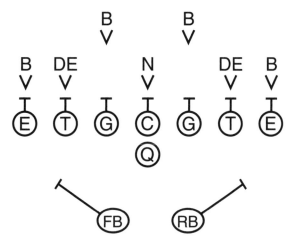

Figure 11.9 Max protection against an odd defense

tion of the pass protection (see fig. 11.10). He will usually go to the strong side of the formation. The back to the weak side of the formation will be responsible for picking up the inside backer to that side. The back to the front-side is there to help or pick up any blitz from the secondary.

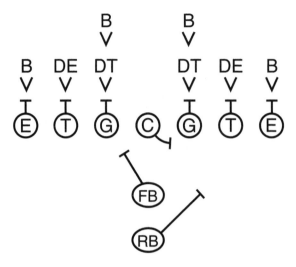

Figure 11.10 Max protection against an even defense

Bootleg Protection

Bootlegs passes are used as a misdirection play against the defense. The quarterback fakes a handoff to one side and then rolls out to the other side to throw the pass. The idea is to get the backers flowing in the wrong direction, making it easier to get a receiver open. The uncovered linemen usually pull out in front of the quarterback to give him protection.

Against an odd front, one of the key blocks is that of the front-side tackle (see fig. 11.11). His job is to keep the defensive end on the line of scrimmage and not let him get to the outside. This block is similar to the play action protection (see Chapter 12), except you don't have to be as aggressive. The defensive end should read flow away and want to work to the inside. Keep him flat on the line but let him move to the inside. When he reads bootleg, he will want to work back to the right. This is when you pin him inside. The worst thing that can happen is to get beaten quickly to the inside, so do not favor the outside by over-setting to the outside. Also try to preread the stance and body lean of the defensive end to give you a hint which side he is likely to charge. If there is ever a doubt, don't get beaten to the inside.

As the quarterback rolls to the outside, try to keep your butt to the quarterback and stay between him and the defensive end. The front-side guard can

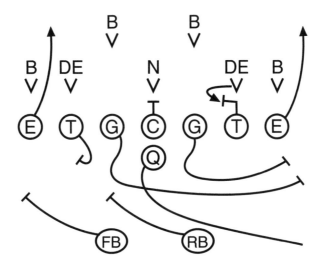

Figure 11.11 Bootleg protection against an odd defense

step left to show flow, then should take a flat step to the outside like when pulling and then get depth. His job will be to hook or log the outside linebacker. The outside backer will react to the play action away from him by either coming flat down the line or starting to go behind the line of scrimmage to make the play that is being faked to the other side. If he is coming flat down the line, the guard needs to get depth quickly and log him in. If he is going behind the line of scrimmage, he is running himself out of the play and the guard can look for other people to block. If he is blitzing hard on the play, the guard has a very tough assignment. He still needs to log him to the inside, but the biggest problem is to stop the penetration the backer is getting. To stop this penetration, the guard should hit the backer with his inside shoulder at hip height, getting his head in front of the backer to stop the penetration. If he cannot get across the backer, then the quarterback has to read this and pull up and stop the boot action to the outside.

The center will block the nose man, essentially like a cutoff block on a running play. The nose should read the flow of the play away, making the block a little easier. The back-side guard may make a false step left to show flow, then should pull and follow the front-side guard. If the front-side guard gets the log block, he can then continue to the outside, looking for anyone who may show. If the front-side guard does not get the log block and the quarterback has to pull

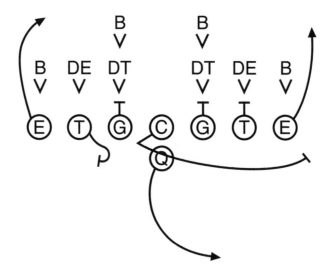

Figure 11.12 Bootleg protection against an even defense

up, he should look to the back side for any pressure coming from there. The back-side tackle has a cutoff-type block on the defensive end over him.

Against an even defense, there will be only one man who can get out on the boot (see fig. 11.12). The front-side guard and tackle will do the cutoff-type blocks as the tackle did against the odd front as described previously. If the back-side guard can get the cutoff-type block on the defensive tackle over him, then the center will pull down the line of scrimmage to get the log block on the outside backer as the front-side guard did against the odd front. If the defensive tackle is in the gap between the guard and center, then you can have the center block back on him and have the back-side guard be the man that pulls and logs the outside backer.

In any situation described in this chapter, when a player is looking to the outside for a blitzer, expecting it to be a backer, and if a backer does not come, before he turns back in he should look to see if there is a cornerback blitzing from the outside. This is common sense, and since linemen are the smartest players on the field, I am sure they already figured that out.

12

Screens and Play Action

Screen passes can be a very effective way of getting the ball into the hands of the running back with blockers in front of him and potentially an open field to work with. They are also an effective way to slow down a pass rush. However, screen passes take a lot of work to run properly. The timing is very difficult, and it takes much practice time to run them effectively.

I did not run many screens either in college or with the Giants because neither coach thought the amount of time necessary to do them effectively was worth the potential gains. We would have one or two screens in the game plan and run one about every other game. There are teams that will have as many as ten screens in the plan and run about that many each game. It depends on your personnel and how much time you want to devote to them.

The basic screen has the running back stay in the backfield as if he was picking up a blitzer, then after about two seconds he releases into the flat. One or two linemen will get off their blocks and get in front of him to lead him downfield. It sounds simple, as most football plays do conceptually, but many components have to come together to have a successful play.

The front-side tackle has one of the tougher blocks on this play. He must invite his man upfield to a depth of about six yards. At that point, the back is about ready to release. The tackle should cut the rusher, getting him to the ground. The reason for this is twofold: first, to make sure the rusher does not grab the back as he releases into the flat, and second, to give the quarterback a clear view of the back and give him a throwing lane. When the rusher gets to the mark about six yards upfield, the tackle should work to get a slight separation from him, and then do a cut block, aiming his inside shoulder for the outside thigh of the rusher. Drive through the thigh, following with your body to hit the inside leg as well. This should get the rusher to the ground, or at worst, get his hands down so the quarterback can complete the pass.

There are many things that can go wrong with this block. If you get too much separation, the rusher can read the cut block coming, push the tackle to the ground, and jump into the pass lane and either bat the ball down or intercept the pass. If the tackle misses the cut block, it leaves the rusher to get in the face of the passer, or he may read the play and tackle the back or follow him into the flat to not allow the pass to be completed. If the rusher takes an inside move, this makes the tackle's job easy—he just rides him in and keeps him out of the play. The tackle should try to have his man avoid the other linemen who are trying to get out on the screen.

The back-side tackle should just block his man as if it was a normal passing play. The tendency is to relax because he is away from the play side and knows that the quarterback should be getting the ball off in about two-and-a-half or three seconds. If the timing of the play gets thrown off, however, the quarterback will need time to adjust, so the tackle must approach this as any other pass play and block just as hard.

The guards and center have the potentially fun blocks on the play. Generally two of the three interior linemen will release out into the flat, after blocking for about two seconds to lead the back on the screen. The front-side guard generally releases with either the center or back-side guard, whoever was uncovered by a defensive lineman at the snap.

The uncovered lineman has the easiest job. He takes his normal pass set and looks for a blitzer, generally an inside linebacker. After a count of two, he releases into the flat to lead the back after he catches the ball.

The covered lineman must block his man for a count of two, and then make it appear that he gets beaten so the man goes in to rush the quarterback. After his man "beats" him, the lineman will then release into the flat. Very often, the covered lineman gets in a hurry and barely blocks the rusher, letting the man into the backfield too soon and rushing the quarterback on the play. He must block his man for a full two seconds before releasing him or the timing on the play will not work. Ideally, you want the lineman to get "beaten" to the inside

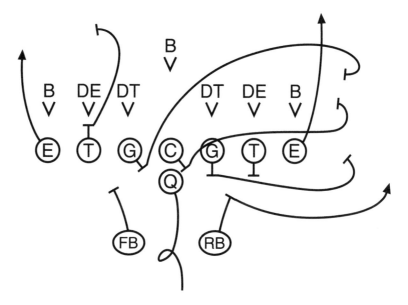

Figure 12.1 Screen pass blocking (high school)

so he has a clean release into the flat. If the rusher beats him to the outside, he will feel the blocker go behind him, letting him know it is a screen. The best way to get beaten is to overset the rusher to the outside, allowing him an inside lane. But the block must be held for the two-count first. Dropping your head or allowing the man into your body will generally help you get "beaten."

The rules for going downfield on a pass completed behind the line of scrimmage vary. For high school and college the linemen can release on the snap of the ball and can block at any time (see fig. 12.1). At the pro level linemen cannot go downfield until the pass is thrown and cannot block until the pass is completed (see fig. 12.2 on the next page).

As the linemen release, they should stay close to the line of scrimmage. When the back catches the ball, he will yell "go," informing the linemen that he has the ball and they can safely go past the line of scrimmage to make their blocks. At the pro level the linemen releasing cannot go downfield until they hear the "go" because pressure may have been put on the quarterback or the back might have been caught up getting out to the flat. (At the high school level the linemen can go downfield anytime.)

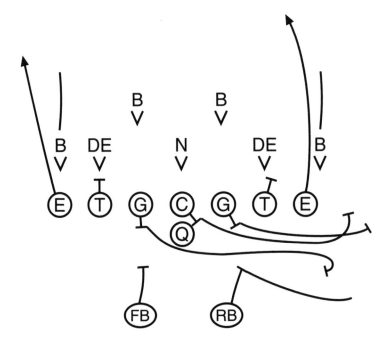

Figure 12.2 Screen pass blocking (pro)

The first lineman to get out on the screen will block the backer or safety that is responsible for the back that is releasing. That should be the first person to show. The second man will first turn and look to the inside for anyone coming from there. If no one shows, then he will turn upfield and block the first opposite-colored jersey he finds.

We have detailed many things that could go wrong on a screen. But if done properly, you have the ball in the hands of your most effective ball carrier in the open field with at least one blocker in front of him. Many goods things can happen, but it will take a lot of practice time to become efficient at this play.

Play Action Passes

Play action passes are an effective way of holding the linebackers so you can get a receiver behind them and in front of the defensive back. On this type of play, you fake a running play into the line to hold the linebackers. Just faking with the back will not hold the backer, though. The linemen also need to fake run blocking initially for the backers to bite. On the side to which you are faking the run, this is relatively easy. The tackle will initiate a drive block on the man over him. He should come out low into the defender just like a drive block, but under control, aiming to hit the defender on the inside number to keep inside protection. Once contact is made, instead of then driving the hips and legs into the block and trying to get backward motion, push out with the arms to get separation, bring the head back, and drop the butt to get into a good pass protection position. It is very important to get the hands in on this block initially because you will start out in the bad position of being body-to-body with the defender. If the backer sees the tackle's head pop up at all, it will tell him that the run is a fake, so a good effort must be given on the initial hit. The biggest problem with this block is if the defender is slanting. It is easy to miss the man or not get very much of him if you are too aggressive on the block. It is better to be a little tentative on the initial hit, but do it with your head low. Scouting of opponents, knowing how often they slant, when this may be, and if they tip off their slants will greatly help the tackle in knowing how to approach this block.

The back that the ball is being faked to will be responsible for the first backer on the play side. The quarterback will set up at a point behind the play-side guard. The linemen need to keep this in mind, knowing what their protection point is. It is no longer behind the center.

If the front-side guard is covered, he will use the same technique as the front-side tackle, simulating a drive block and then going into pass protection mode. If he is uncovered, he will make it look like he is blocking down, but actually he will be the initial person starting slide protection to the back side. He will also want to stay low into this block, making it look like a true drive block, then pull up and get into good pass protection position. The center and back-side guard will also appear to be blocking back for the run, staying low. The three middle linemen will also be responsible for any blitzes that come from the back side, with the uncovered man, after first simulating a run-type block, looking out for and intercepting any blitzer.

The back-side tackle has a tough job. He will block the last man on the line of scrimmage on the back side. This sometimes will be a linebacker, usually a good athlete. Quite often, the pass pattern run with a play action pass will have a slant or in-cut run by the back-side wide receiver. Normally the back-side backer would be responsible for this area, so it is important to get a good run fake at this backer to hold him. The tackle should take at least one if not two or three hard steps at the backer to keep him close to the line of scrimmage. The danger in this is that if the backer is blitzing, the tackle will not be in a good position to take him on because he is moving toward him with his head low. Once again, knowing the defensive tendencies will greatly help the tackle. If the backer is blitzing, he will not be responsible for the area behind him and does not have to be fooled into not dropping off on the play. But you can still influence the person who does have that coverage, so an effort should be made not to show pass immediately. Take one step at the backer, but then get in pass protection position. If the backer is coming, it is more important to block him than to sell the play. If you have a person like Lawrence Taylor out there who blitzes about 90 percent of the time, forget about selling the run. Just block him. If he is not coming, take three good hard steps at him to try to hold him. Check for any blitzers coming from the outside, and if none show, turn back inside and help one of your teammates.

13

Fundamentals for the Snapper

The center, or snapper, is the most important lineman on most offensive lines. (In the rules the person we usually call the center is called the snapper. He snaps the ball to get the play started.) The center should be a leader and for many teams will be the best blocker. Snapping the ball is an extremely important fundamental. The play can't get started if the ball is not snapped properly.

The Center Snap

The snapper's stance utilizes the same principles as the other offensive linemen. If he is to angle block and cup pass protect he should be more balanced. If he is going forward most of the time he will have more weight forward. The center may have only one hand down, the one that's on the ball, or may have one hand on the ball and the other on the ground for support. The four-point center stance is more useful when the center is blocking straight ahead on quick plays.

Only the center can be in the line of scrimmage. The line of scrimmage is actually a zone bounded by two planes. The planes extend from each end of the ball, parallel with the goal lines and as wide as the sidelines. The planes extend from the ground to the sky. Consequently any player, other than the center, who puts his head or arm into that zone is offside if the ball is snapped while he is in that zone. In high school football merely putting any part of the body into that zone, even if the ball isn't snapped, is a penalty. This penalty is called *encroachment* and is a five-yard penalty.

Snapping the Ball

The method of snapping the ball will be determined by how the coach wants the quarterback to take it. Most teams have the snapper turn the ball as it moves from the ground to the quarterback's hands.

In coaching the snap, start with the ball in the quarterback's hands just exactly as he wants to take it—usually with the laces across the fingers of his passing hand. From this "perfect" position the snapper reaches up and takes the ball from the quarterback and puts it on the ground. Note where the laces are. This is where they should be before the snap. Most right-handed centers will find that they must start with the laces an eighth to a quarter of a turn to the left from being straight up.

The quarterback will usually have his passing hand well into the crotch of the center, giving upward pressure on the center's crotch. His wrists should be together. His other hand should be at a 90-degree or greater angle so that the snap will not hit his fingers, which are pointing at the ground. The quarterback should give forward pressure with his top wrist as the center moves into his block as he snaps the ball.

When the center comes to the line of scrimmage and assumes his pre-snap stance he should adjust the ball so that it will be just the way he wants if for the snap. The referee will generally place the ball with the laces straight up. The center should adjust the ball by placing all five fingers on the near end of the ball and twisting it until the laces are where he wants them. By adjusting the ball this way he will not ever be penalized for attempting to draw the opponents offside with a false snap. This type of penalty is more likely to be called if the player puts his hand on top of the ball and then twists or moves it.

When the laces are properly positioned the snapper should put his hand on the ball and slowly tip it to whatever angle he desires for the snap (see photo 13.1). Once this angle is achieved he should not move the ball lest a penalty be called for attempting to draw his opponents offside.

The T-Formation Snap

The T-formation snap should be as fast as the center can make it. Strong latissimus dorsi and triceps muscles are necessary for a hard snap. The snapper should drive the ball hard up into his crotch where the quarterback's hands are waiting (see photo 13.2). The snapper should be stepping into his block as he snaps the ball. It is not "snap, then block," but rather "block while snapping." Since the snapper is moving as he snaps the ball, the quarterback must move his hands forward with the snapper until he knows for certain that he has the ball. Many fumbles occur because either the snapper has slowed his arm movement as the ball approached the quarterback's hands or the quarterback has pulled his hands away before he had control of the snap.

The Long Snap

The long snap used in single-wing offenses and in shotgun attacks is much more difficult to master. In this snap the positioning of the laces in the pre-snap adjustment should be for the comfort of the snapper, not the quarterback. Usually the

Photo 13.1 Ready to snap

Photo 13.2 The snap

right-handed snapper will turn the laces at least a quarter-turn clockwise (to his right). He will take a grip as if he were passing the ball.

The snapper can use a one- or a two-hand snap. For a one-hand snap he merely passes the ball between his legs. If using a two-hand snap he will put his nonpower hand (the left hand for right-handed snappers) on top of the ball. It will be there simply to guide the ball. Using two hands is more likely to give a straight pass because the shoulders are forced to stay even. If only one hand is on the ball the right shoulder may drop and the ball may drift left. However, the one-hand snap is more often used so that the nonsnapping hand can be ready for contacting the defender in the block.

At the lower levels of football the snapper should look at his target (see photos 13.3 and 13.4). It is generally best to aim the snap at the thighs rather than at chest height. During the excitement of the game the snapper is likely to make his mistakes as high snaps. A snap aimed at the thighs that is three feet too high is not problem, but a snap aimed at the shoulders that is three feet too high may result in a large loss on the play.

At the higher levels of play the snapper may practice the blind snap, in which he looks at his blocking target rather than at the target of his snap. It is even more important to aim the ball low when snapping blind because the chance of missing the target is much greater when the snapper isn't looking at it.

Photo 13.3 Young snappers should look at their target.

Photo 13.4 Follow-through

Cadence and the Snap Count

The snap count should be geared to getting the offensive players starting at the same instant. A secondary consideration is to fool the defense. Teams that vary their snap counts from play to play may fool the defense two ways. If they generally go on 2, the second count, they may sometimes go on 1, the first count, and catch the defenders not quite ready to play. Or they may go on 3, hoping that the defenders will jump offside on the second count because they expected the ball to be snapped earlier.

The number of syllables in a snap count is important for the offense. While some teams use only a single syllable, such as "go," "hike," or "hut," other teams will use a two-syllable count such as "hu-two" (hut two), and other teams will use a three-syllable count such as "a-hu-two" (a hut two) or "re-dee-go" (ready go). Dr. Fred Miller, former athletic director at San Diego State University, did his master's thesis on snap counts. He found that the three-count snap got the offensive linemen firing off more quickly on the ball. Apparently the three syllables alerted them to the snap count more effectively.

The snapper is responsible for getting the ball into play at the exact instant called by the quarterback. Some coaches want the ball in the hands of the quarterback as the snap count is called. Others want the line moving just before the ball is snapped. So if the snap count is "a-hut-two" the line may go on "hut" and the ball be snapped on "two."

Rhythmic and nonrhythmic cadences are also a consideration when determining your approach to the snap count. In a rhythmic cadence the counts are equally spaced, such as "go—go—go—go." in a nonrhythmic cadence the pauses between the counts will vary. So a nonrhythmic count might be "go————go—go————go." It is hoped that by using nonrhythmic cadences the quarterback may be able to get the defense to jump offside. Some quarterbacks do this very well by varying the tones of their voices. For example, if the snap count is on 3 but he calls the second count louder than normal, the defense may jump.

Should you vary the snap count? A number of years ago the number one team in the nation went on the first snap count every play of the season. The coach didn't want his players making a mistake, so he never varied the count. Several college coaches used this reasoning recently. Some coaches will use a long count and nearly always go on the last sound, but may occasionally go on an earlier sound hoping to get the jump on the defense that is used to having the ball snapped on the last sound.

An example would be a cadence in which the quarterback would say "set . . . down . . . hike . . . ready go." At least 90 percent of the plays would start on the "ready go" count. It would be understood that if no snap was called in the huddle "ready go" would be the snap count. With this in mind no offensive player should ever move before hearing "ready go." There should therefore never be an offensive offside or motion penalty—consequently a major potential offensive mistake would be eliminated. However the ball might be snapped earlier, perhaps giving the offense a small advantage over the defense that had become used to going on the "ready go" command. If the play is called on an earlier count than "ready go," the worst that should happen to the offense is that an unalert player would be late in starting—but that would not cause a penalty.

With the Giants, our cadence consisted of the quarterback saying a color, then a number, repeating those again, then "hut—hut." We generally went on either the first or second "hut." If we had a third and less than five yards, we would sometimes go on the third "hut," but if we tried this Phil Simms would stress that it was going to be on 3 before he called the play. Even then we would screw it up about 10 percent of the time and go early—and we were pros. Keep it simple, especially with younger teams.

Also, if a player breaks the huddle and is unsure of the snap count, he should always ask another player what it is, even if the defense hears him. It is better for the defense to know the snap count than have a five-yard penalty.

Remember that a major part of coaching is eliminating mistakes. If you can eliminate all offside and motion penalties by the offense you have made a major stride in offensive success because it is very difficult to overcome any offensive penalty.

In using such a multiple-syllable cadence, in this case a four-word cadence, the coach might tie certain offensive responsibilities to each word. For example, the line might break the huddle and align in a two-point stance. On "set" the offense would take their down stance positions. On "down" the backs and/or ends might shift. On "hike" they might use motion if that is part of the play. On "ready go" the ball would be snapped. But if there is no shift or motion the quarterback might have the ball snapped on "set," "down," or "hike." If there is a shift but no motion the ball could be snapped on "hike" or "ready go."

Having the offensive team start in a two-point stance has an advantage. The defensive linemen must be in their down stances (three- or four-point stances) because they know that the ball can be snapped with the offense in a two-point stance. The longer the defenders are in their down stances the more cramped their muscles become and the less likely they will be able to react quickly to the movement of the offense. Consequently having the offense set in two-point stances while the defense is down works as an advantage to the offense.

Shifting from a basic set to a different set, such as a tight T to a wing T or tight ends to split ends, requires the defense to make an adjustment that increases its chances of "blowing" an assignment.

The Punt Snap

The punt snap is probably the most important single fundamental in the whole football game. The punt is a play that should gain an average of at least thirty yards—and a blocked punt is a loss of at least fifty yards (the thirty yards the team did not get on its punt and at least another twenty yards lost when the punt was blocked). A few years ago in a practice game the Giants' starting snapper snapped the ball over the punter's head. On the next punt the second-string long snapper did the same thing. On the third punt the third-string snapper also snapped over the punter's head. All were cut on Monday. At any level, the punt snap has to be perfect.

The snap should get to the punter in 0.6 seconds if the punter is at ten yards, 0.7 seconds if the punter is twelve yards deep, and 0.8 to 0.9 seconds if the punter is at fifteen yards. If the punter gets the punt off in 1.2 seconds there should be little chance of a blocked punt.

The point of aim of the punt snap depends on the consistency and accuracy of the snapper. If his snap is always on target and the punter wants the ball at chest height, then he can put it into the punter's hands. But since most snappers snap high in a game some coaches will have the punter put his hands just inside

Most pro teams now carry a specialist just for punt and field-goal snaps. They may practice the rest of the time with the team as scout team players, but the coaches have no intentions of putting most of them in the game except for their specialty. There have been guys who have played in the NFL for ten years or more without being on the field except for the times they snap the ball. You can have a long and profitable career if you can deep snap—but like a kicker, if you screw up in a big situation, you will be out of a job even before you get back to the sidelines.

of the knee of the kicking leg. If the snapper aims at the punter's knee and gets it there it does not slow up the punter. However if he makes a bad snap and hits it three feet too high, it still will land near the punter's chest—so there is no problem. If we are trying to eliminate mistakes the low snap makes more sense.

Competent coaches should have a stopwatch on their snappers weekly. Snappers should have a target painted on a wall at home so they have a chance to practice daily on making the perfect snap.

The blind snap is the objective of effective high school and college snappers. This takes much more work to perfect—and there will nearly always be more errors in hitting the exact target. Yet practice makes perfect, so it can be done. The snapper who can make the perfect blind snap in the minimum amount of time may gain a scholarship just on this one skill.

The ideal snapper will also work to eliminate the natural tendency to raise the hips just as he is starting his snap. This raising of the hips gives alert punt blockers about a 0.2 second jump in getting started in their charge to block the punt.

The Field Goal Snap

The field goal snap is a bit different from the punt snap in that the placing of the laces is very important to the kicker. If the holder can get the ball in his hands perfectly, or nearly perfectly, so that he doesn't have to turn the laces far to get a perfect hold (a hold with the laces pointing directly at the goalposts), the kick can be made more accurately and more quickly.

To do this the holder should place himself exactly where he will be in a game—seven to eight yards behind the snapper. Seven yards has been traditional, but in college and at the pro level, as more field goals are being blocked by tall leapers, more coaches are moving the holder back a yard or so. With the holder at his game depth the snapper will snap ten snaps starting with the laces straight up. After ten snaps the holder should be able to tell, within an inch or two, where the laces will land. If they are landing at about a three o'clock position, have the snapper start with the laces at nine o'clock. Wherever the ball is being caught, there will be an adjustment that the snapper can make in the ball's starting position so that it will land in the holder's hands almost perfectly every time—with the laces upward, at twelve o'clock.

The target point should be twelve to eighteen inches directly over the tee. Making the holder reach in any direction for the ball can disturb the timing of the kick and result in a failed kick. Just as in the punt, it is the snapper who is most likely to create variables in the timing of the kick—and a few hundredths of a second on the hold can delay the timing of the kicker and force him to kick poorly. Often the kicker is blamed for a poor kick when it is the fault of the snapper or the holder.

Choosing to Be the Snapper

If you choose to become the snapper you must have confidence in yourself and be willing to work harder than any other lineman. If you are also going to be a long snapper your work effort will be doubled as you perfect your long snapping skills. If you have the dedication and the leadership skills—and you are willing to be the hardest-working person on your team, you can be a snapper.

14

Blocking for the Kicking Game

The kicking teams or "special teams" comprise almost 25 percent of a typical game of football, but are often overlooked or ignored by coaches. You may give special teams five minutes at the start or at the end of practice if you are a typical coach, but do you give only five minutes to your passing game or inside running game? There will probably be more special teams plays in a typical game than passing or inside running plays, so you should give them their due.

Offensive linemen are generally not involved with all aspects of special teams. We will cover punt protection and coverage, PAT and field goal protection, and kickoff return. Generally punt return is done by the defense, as is often PAT and field goal block. Kickoff coverage is done also by the defense and the faster players on offense.

Punt Protection Blocking

The punt is the most important play in football. It can gain thirty to fifty yards, and a blocked punt can give up from fifteen yards to a touchdown.

There are several approaches to blocking for the punt. The current fad seems to be copied from the pros. At the professional level only the two outside "gunners" are allowed to go downfield before the ball is punted (see fig. 14.1). This,

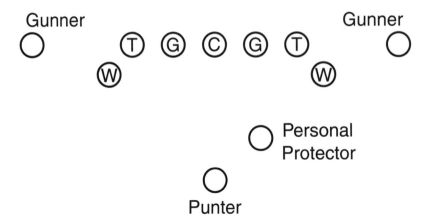

Figure 14.1 Pro-style punt formation with two outside gunners

of course, is to increase the opportunity for a punt return—which should make the game more exciting. The most common formation has the guards and tackles in their normal positions with two wingbacks and a personal protector.

The guards take a six-inch split from the snapper. The toe of the guard's inside foot should align with the heel of the snapper. The tackles align even with the guards but with a foot split. The wings align about a yard deep with the inside foot on a line with the tackle's outside foot. All will be in a two-point stance with the outside foot back. From this position the offensive lineman will take two steps back and pick up any rusher. By taking two steps back there is a good chance that any planned defensive stunt will be evident and can be blocked. Stunts are much more difficult to block effectively when the linemen stay on the line of scrimmage to make their blocks.

Upon the snap of the ball, the linemen and the wings will take two "kick slide" steps backward. The kick slide step is very similar to the step taken by an offensive tackle to get depth when he has a rusher to his outside, except that here the lineman must work straight back instead of gaining some width. The first step is a push-off step with the inside foot to get moving backward. The Giants special teams coach, Mike Sweatman, calls this the *power toe*. The foot must be pointed directly forward or even slightly inside in the stance to get the best push-off. The lineman should try to move about a foot backward with this step. The outside foot shuffles back to keep the same toe-to-heel relationship with the inside foot that it had at the snap. A second set of steps should then be taken, then the inside foot steps directly back.

From this point the lineman waits for whoever enters his zone, which is from his inside shoulder to the inside shoulder of the next man out. As the defender enters his zone he punches out with his elbows in and the fingers upward. It is possible that two defenders can enter his zone. In this case the lineman can hit one with one arm and the other with the other arm.

The guard is responsible for the area from the cheek of the center to the nose of the tackle. The tackle is responsible for the area from his nose to the nose of the end. The end is responsible from his nose to the nose of the wing. The wing is responsible from his nose to the outside rusher.

As the linemen slide back they stab with their inside arm to cover their most inside responsibility. Their outside arm will go up to protect their most outside responsibility. Since this is zone protection, a man may have to block two people if they both come to his responsible area.

Some teams use man protection rather than zone blocking. A common rule for blocking men is to number them from the inside out on each side of the ball. In man protection the guard will take the number one man, the tackle the number two, and the wing the number three. But many teams number from the outside in with the widest man taking the one man, and so on.

Once the block is made and the thud of the kick is heard, the offensive lineman releases downfield to cover the kick. On the coverage the snapper and gunners will be downfield first. The guards, tackles, and wings will cover about four to five yards apart, always keeping the ball inside them. The widest coverage players must make certain that they contain any possible ball carrier. If there is a wide man who might receive a lateral pass, the wide man has to protect against this. If there are two punt returners and they cross, either reversing or faking the reverse, each offensive player must tackle the player coming at him.

Another common punt formation is the older spread punt (see fig. 14.2 on the next page). In this formation two backs are set in the two- to three-foot center-guard gaps. The tackles split two to three yards from the guards, and the ends are split another three feet.

In this formation there is more of a chance that the coach will use man blocking. Often the rule is to block the defender on or outside. However some will count defenders, either from the inside out or the outside in (see fig. 14.3 on the next page).

Another formation is the tackles back spread punt (see fig. 14.4 on page 123). This formation allows the faster players to play in the offensive line for coverage while setting the bull elephants back to absorb the rushers who are able to break through the line and are honestly trying to block the punt.

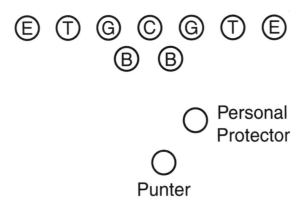

Figure 14.2 Spread punt formation

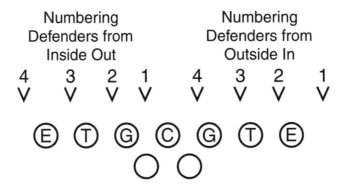

Figure 14.3 Counting defenders in a punt formation

Whatever the formation or type of protection, the offensive lineman must be ready to fight through any defender who is holding him up and attempting to set up a return. He can head fake, bull rush, or swim to get free, then get to the proper width for his punt coverage.

The center has one job: snap the ball back to the punter as quickly and as accurately as possible. With the punter at ten yards the snap should get to him in about six-tenths of a second. It is best to aim at the punter's knee because in a game the snap is often high because of the snapper's excitement. Since the

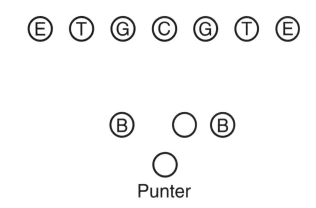

Figure 14.4 Tackles back spread punt

snapper cannot be hit by a defender until his head is up, there is no reason to fear a defender. (In earlier days it was legal to hit the snapper while his head was still down. Wise rule makers have eliminated that move.) After the snap, he should take a shuffle step or two backward and try to make himself as big as possible to stop the rushers coming right over him.

The splits taken vary by position. The guards should have their inside foot almost directly behind the feet of the snapper. They must be careful of two things: that they do not get their feet in the way of the snap and that they do not hinder the snapper's motion. Often the snapper will push back with his feet to get the snap back quickly. Make sure he has room to do this. The splits between the guard and tackle and the tackle and end should be about one foot. For this discussion, we will assume that the ends will be in, by the tackles, and not split out like the pros. This will make the blocking easier and widen the spot where a blocker has to turn the corner. Younger players usually are not as accurate in getting the ball back, so the block point (the spot where the punter's foot will meet the ball) can vary by a few feet. Having the ends in gives added protection and room for error. The wings should line up with their inside foot just beyond the outside foot of the end.

The men on the line should all take the same type of stance. They should have their feet shoulder width apart or even a little narrower, with the inside foot up and the toe of the outside foot at the depth of the heel of the inside foot. Hands should be on the thighs. Shoulders should be down, with the player bent at the waist forming a 45-degree angle between his upper body and the ground. This is to help stop a bull rush and also to stop the blocker from getting grabbed.

You should know how long it takes from the time the ball is snapped until it is kicked. In the pros, this is usually just over two seconds, so the players are taught to block for two seconds and then go downfield to cover the kick. If your punt takes longer, have the blockers block longer. You must also know your punter's block point. In the pros, with the punter back fifteen yards from the snapper, it is generally nine-and-a-half to ten yards from the line of scrimmage, but yours might vary from this. Make sure that the linemen know what point they are protecting.

Once the ball is kicked, the blockers become cover men. The linemen need to fan out as they cover so as to not leave holes for the returner to run to. The center will go straight downfield if the kick is straight downfield. The punter should call right, left, or middle and deep or short to adjust the middle of the coverage team to the ball. The guards should run down about six yards to either side of the center. The tackles should be six yards outside of the guards. The ends should be six yards outside the tackles. The wingmen will be your ball hawks, going directly to the ball. If you wish, you can have your ends and wingmen switch assignments between the being widest man on the fan-out and being the ball hawks.

A good way to practice the fanning out is to have cones or towels about fifteen yards downfield and six yards apart. These are generally called *landmarks*. On the snap of the ball, the blockers should do their kick slide steps, then run downfield to cover, making sure they run to the proper cone or towel to get the feel of where they should be.

Field Goal and Point-After-Touchdown (PAT) Blocking

Most coaches put their offensive linemen on the field goal team—in the five interior positions and possibly even at the ends. The major difference between field goal protection and PAT protection is that the rushers usually come harder on the PAT. There is more possibility for the fake on a field goal attempt. It is nearly universal to have the guards overlap their feet with the snapper. There should be no splits between the linemen. The blockers must not move their inside leg. Their primary responsibility is to block a man coming to their inside gap. Some coaches will have their linemen put their heads into the hip of the next lineman in. It looks somewhat like a row of elephants at the circus, so it is often called the *elephant block*. At the higher levels of play it is more common to have the tackles and ends step behind the man inside to reduce any chance of defenders coming inside.

The center is the key to this team. His only job is to get the ball back to the holder as fast as possible to the exact spot that the holder wants it. The center can take any stance he wants in order to get the job done. With practice he can even get the laces facing forward so the holder doesn't have to spin the ball too far.

The guards line up next to the center. The guard should take his inside foot and put it directly behind the foot of the center. His outside foot will be the forward foot in his stance. The feet should be slightly wider than shoulder width. The wider the stances are for the linemen, the wider the corner will be for the wide rushers coming around. The guards should put their inside hand down in their stance. Their heads should be up and turned to the inside so they can see the snap of the ball. Upon the snap, the guards will step with their inside foot about six to twelve inches and brace the center's legs with their thighs. This is very important because the center has his head down, and when he snaps the ball he is defenseless and needs to be braced. The outside foot must not move. Also at the snap the guards should raise their outside arms, bent at the elbow, so that their forearm is at shoulder level protecting the outside gap.

The tackles should line up their inside foot behind the outside foot of the guards and have their inside hand down with square shoulders and head slightly turned to the inside to see the snap of the ball. On the snap they will do the same step and arm action described for the guards.

The ends should line up the same as the guards and tackles. On the snap they will take the same inside step, but then take a hinge step with the outside foot, moving it back about twelve inches while getting the outside arm up.

The wing lines up on the hip of the end, off the ball and facing at a 45-degree angle to the line of scrimmage. His most important job is to protect the inside. Once the inside is secure, then he can redirect the outside rusher wide enough to not block the kick. The weakest point is generally the gap between the end and the wing. The wing must be prepared to block two men, hitting any inside rusher with his inside hand and any outside rusher with his outside hand.

The kick should be away in about 1.4 seconds, so any delay of the rushers will probably prevent them from blocking it.

Kickoff Return Blocking

For the kickoff, most teams run their blockers back to a point ten to fifteen yards in front of the ball. They extend an arm outward to the next player to ensure a two- to three-foot gap between them. They then move forward together as a wall or wedge. Some coaches will also send a trapper just outside the wedge hoping that the runner can escape the wedge and get additional yardage.

Some teams will block assigned men. Usually they will drop back in front of the ball carrier, then move forward attacking the potential tacklers. The block will generally be with hand contact but can be with the shoulder if the contact is made above the waist. Another approach for return blockers is to run with the potential tackler, slowly reducing the gap between them so that by the time they are about ten yards from the ball carrier the blocker will hit into the chest of the potential tackler.

The positioning of the players for the kickoff return team has changed over the years. It used to be that the linemen were the men who lined up ten to fifteen yards from the ball. They would drop back and try to make open field blocks against much smaller and quicker men. This doesn't make much sense. Now, it is the smaller and faster guys who are the "up" men, with the big guys in the wedge, leading the ball carrier.

The wedge is the most common type of kickoff return used. There are two basic returns: wedge right and wedge left.

The alignment for the return will be to have five up men between ten and fifteen yards from the kickoff point, evenly spaced across the field, with the widest men well outside the numbers. The tackles will be lined up about the width of the numbers. The depth will depend on how far you expect the kick to travel. Generally the tackles will be five yards in front of the fullbacks. The fullbacks should line up at the width of the hash marks, but may be as tight as ten yards apart. They should be about fifteen yards in front of where you expect the kick to go to. That leaves two deep men to field the kick.

We will number the coverage men from the outside in, so in a balanced kickoff situation, R1 would be the outside man on the right side and L5 would be the man closest to the kicker on the left side. We will describe a return to the left.

The up men will watch for an onside kick, dropping back only when they see the ball go over their heads. They will drop about fifteen yards, then block their assigned men, pushing them out to the right by getting their heads on the left sides of their men and driving them toward the sidelines. The left end will block L4, the left guard will block L5, the center will block R5, the right guard will block R4, and the right end will block R3.

The tackles and fullbacks will form the wedge twelve to fifteen yards in front of the spot where the ball will be caught. One person will be designated the captain of the wedge, usually the right fullback. He will run to the spot twelve to fifteen yards in front of the catch point. The other three members of the wedge will join him there. They will turn to face upfield and wait for the captain to yell "go" as soon as the ball is caught. They will then lead the ball carrier to the left and up the field. It is a good idea to have the players in the wedge hold hands as they run upfield leading the carrier. This will keep them in a tight formation. They can run holding hands, but they must let go before they make contact with any cover men. The wedge should have a four-on-three situation, picking up L1, L2, and L3. They will also pick up anyone who breaks through the blocks of the up men. Blocking in the wedge is just old-fashioned determination. They will be hitting guys running at them at about full speed. But since you have your bigger men in the wedge and the coverage guys are usually smaller, the wedge should have the advantage. As the wedge takes on the cover men, the wedge players should hit them with their shoulders and hands, just as if they were blocking a backer or defensive back in the open field. The wedge should just run through these smaller players. All blocks must be made above the waist. A common practice years ago was to have a "wedge buster" come down and go in low on the wedge, knocking down as many of them as he could. This is now illegal for safety reasons.

The returner who does not get the ball will secure the back side and pick up the most dangerous cover man.

15

Strength and Anaerobic Conditioning

When we talk about strength training, we must include power. Offensive linemen need power, which is the combination of speed and strength. To develop power you must use less weight in your strength training, but do the action faster. Speed is best developed by working at about 40 percent of your one-repetition maximum.

Most weight lifting athletes do approximately ten repetitions of the exercises in their workouts. There is nothing wrong with doing ten repetitions as long as the lifter exhausts his muscles. Whether you do one, five, ten, or more repetitions, the key is to exhaust your muscles to the point that you absolutely cannot do even one more repetition.

I do not recommend heavy lifting until high school, unless the athlete is a very early developer. The body of the athlete must be ready for lifting and strength training. I was a late developer, and I could have lifted all day at age twelve and not gotten the same out of it as someone who had matured earlier. Lifting should be done in an organized and supervised setting only, especially with young lifters.

Strength

Your strength is determined by how much weight you can lift one time—but not two. This is your one-repetition maximum. If you are working on speed you would work at 40 percent of your one-repetition maximum and work to exhaustion.

Strength, power, and speed are determined by a combination of your muscles and your brain. In your muscles you have many thousands of small units, called *sarcomeres*, which contract your muscles. These contracting units may be fast-twitch fibers (type 2B), slow-twitch fibers (type 1), or fibers that are intermediate between the fast and the slow (type 2A). The fast-twitch fibers have much more strength but fatigue very quickly. The slow-twitch fibers are not strong but have great endurance. The intermediate fibers are partway between the fast, easily fatigued fibers and the slow-contracting but high-endurance fibers. The fast-twitch fibers are between five and twenty-five times faster and stronger than the slow-twitch fibers. The intermediate fibers lie between the other two in terms of speed, strength, and fatigability.

The types of exercises you do can change the number of each type of fiber in your muscles. Running a long distance will increase the percentage of slow-twitch fibers, while working at a one-repetition maximum or running short sprints will increase the number of fast-twitch fibers, which are the ones you want for football.

Anaerobic Endurance

A brief description of how energy is generated for football is necessary to understand how it can be improved or harmed. The energy in the muscle cell results when one phosphate is released from the adenosine triphosphate (ATP) molecule. The energy released allows the actin and myocin in the sarcomere (the smallest part of the contracting unit in a muscle) to move up on each other. The muscle shortens when enough sarcomeres contract. There is enough ATP in the muscle to supply energy for about three to five seconds (with some estimates for some people as high as ten seconds), before the supply is exhausted. Creatine phosphate in the muscle supplies the energy to resynthesize the ATP by breaking off its phosphate. There is enough creatine phosphate in the muscle to resynthesize ATP (put back a phosphate molecule) for another eight to twenty seconds. There should be more than four times as much creatine as ATP. A series of short sprints works to make this energy system more efficient by increasing the enzymes that make it happen.

The energy sources of ATP and creatine do not use oxygen initially. They are therefore called *anaerobic* or "without oxygen." Football has been found to be about 95 percent anaerobic.

Most strength-power athletes do not have the required amount of creatine phosphate to get maximum performance. The body typically uses up about two grams per day. People on a normal diet eat sufficient amounts of amino acids to make only one gram of creatine per day. People who eat a pound of steak or fish a day probably have enough creatine phosphate to keep a normal balance in the muscle. With enough of the essential amino acids the body may make up to two grams of creatine phosphate per day. Muscle meats supply both the amino acids and the creatine phosphate. However eating a pound or two of meat per day is not as efficient as an energy source because carbohydrates are a more effective energy source than protein. Maximum effective ingestion of protein is between 1.2 and 1.5 grams of protein per kilogram of body weight—or about 2.5 ounces of protein per 100 pounds of body weight.

The best sources of protein in terms of amino acid quality are: egg white (98 percent perfect), skim milk (92 percent perfect), fish (88 percent), chicken, turkey (83 percent), steak (78 percent), soy (72 percent perfect). For the long term health of your heart, fish is far better than chicken or steak because of the omega 3 oils. Chicken or turkey without skin is far better than steak, which contains a great deal of cholesterol and saturated fat.

Anaerobic energy is also created from the use of glucose (blood sugar) and muscle glycogen (simple sugars stored in the muscle). The glycogen action in resynthesizing the ATP starts about three seconds after the beginning of the exercise.

Another energy source that comes into play as a byproduct of the glycogen use is the lactate system. Lactate is produced as the glycogen breaks down into ATP and lactic acid and can interfere with the energy production if it is not effectively removed. However in the trained muscle it can often be reconverted to glycogen or be itself used for energy. Increasing the effectiveness of the lactate removal system is done through repeated 220-yard sprints with short rests—such as jogging a 220 between sprints.

The most common method of reforming the ATP uses oxygen to provide the energy for the process. Using oxygen for energy is called *aerobic*. Oxygen (O_2) begins to become a factor in energy production after a few seconds. It eventually becomes the major factor in long-term continuous exercise.

Let's illustrate the percentage of anaerobic to aerobic sources of energy in middle-distance running events. In tests for a 400-meter run (about 50 to 55 seconds), an 800-meter run (about 1.8 to 2 minutes), and a 1500-meter run (about 4 to 4.5 minutes) it was found that for the 400-meter run about 60 percent of the energy source was anaerobic, for the 800 meters it was about 35 percent, and for the 1500 meters it was 20 percent or less. But remember that football is 95 percent anaerobic. If a substance aids the anaerobic or aerobic process it would help the athlete. Of course if it hurts the process it would be a negative.

While we used to do endurance running for football, we now find that sprinting is more effective in developing the anaerobic energy sources used in football because repeated short sprints help to make the ATP and creatine systems work—probably by increasing the enzymes that aid in the resynthesis of both compounds. Sprints also improve the system that uses blood glucose and muscle glycogen to resynthesize ATP. Longer sprints interspersed with short rests also increase the effectiveness of the lactate removal system.

Running distance, such as a mile or more, for football conditioning works on the aerobic system for generating energy rather than the anaerobic system. It is therefore no longer recommended for football conditioning. Additionally, running distance is more likely to change the intermediate (type 2A) muscle fibers to the slower-reacting and weaker type 1 fibers, so it is a double negative.

Effective Conditioning for Football

We now know that football conditioning needs heavy lifting, fast lifting, and short wind sprints. But weight training is more than just lifting weights. The weights should be lifted in the same posture that you will use in a game. For example, if you are going to be leaning forward in the game, such as in blocking or tackling, you should be leaning forward in your exercise. If you are going to have your elbows close to your body when blocking, they should be close to the body in your exercise.

Consequently, rather than doing a bench press, for example, in the manner that a power lifter would use in a power lifting competition, offensive linemen should do their bench presses with their elbows next to their sides. If you are lifting upward in your block, incline presses would be closer to the angle you will use in the game. If you are pass protecting, the elbows-in bench press would make more sense. But since you can lose up to 50 percent of your power when you shift from the lying posture of a bench press to the upright or leaning forward posture you will use in the game, machines make more sense (see photos 15.1a and 15.1b). Most high-level programs use a machine called the Jammer or Power Thruster to simulate the leaning posture used in a drive block, and any sitting press machine would simulate the posture used in pass protection.

Similarly, while it is typical to do squats for leg strength, their action is vertical and done from two legs. While squats may be ideal for basketball players because they jump vertically in rebounding and in making jump shots, football players use their legs alternately and their push is not vertical but rather at an angle of 20 to 60 degrees from the vertical, depending on the type of block or tackle being done. The Power Runner is a machine that puts the body in a forward leaning position and works the legs alternately, which is a better exercise than squats for football players (see photos 15.2a and 15.2b on the next page).

Photos 15.1a and 15.1b Power Thruster

Photos 15.2a and 15.2b Power Runner

So while any exercise you do will help your playing, some exercises help much more than others. This is probably because your brain learns to stimulate your muscles differently depending on the posture you are in (prone, supine, standing, leaning, and so on) when you perform an action.

Recommended Exercises

This section describes exercises that develop essential muscles used by offensive linemen. We include a variety of exercises for each muscle group, some of which may be done using minimal equipment and others that use specialized machines that may be available to you in a well-equipped program. For more exercises for football conditioning, see *Strength Training Today* by Bob O'Connor and Jerry Simmons of the Carolina Panthers, NFL Strength and Conditioning Coach of the Year in 2003 (published by Wadsworth Publishing).

Neck

The rules of football have been rewritten to take the head out of football. Modern pass protection techniques, and even zone blocking, do not require that the head be a primary instrument in blocking. Yet because football is a contact sport it carries risk, so it is essential to strengthen your neck so you don't injure your cervical vertebrae and spinal column.

Some gyms have head harnesses on which the lifter can hang weights and lift them with the head. And there are some machines, usually isokinetic, that have neck-strength stations. But the simplest way to gain neck strength is to use your own arm strength. With your hands behind your head and your head forward, push your head back, resisting with your arms as much as possible to work the back of the neck (see photo 15.3). (But let your head win the battle!) Next place your hands on your forehead and tilt your head back. Bring your head forward as far as it will go while resisting with your hands to work the front of the neck. Then place your right hand on the right side of your head, allow your head to tilt all the way to the left, then force it right against the resistance of your

Photo 15.3 Exercises for the neck

right arm and hand to work the right side of the neck (see photo 15.3). Repeat the exercise to the left side. Finally, place your right hand against your right temple or jaw and resist while twisting your head until you are looking over your right shoulder. Repeat with left hand at left temple or jaw until looking over your left shoulder. This works the rotary neck muscles that turn the neck.

These same motions can be done with a partner. Lie face down on a bench with your head hanging over and down. Have your partner place resistance on the back of your head while you bring it up over a six count. Do the same for both sides and lying face up.

Upper Chest: Lateral Raise or Fly

The upper chest muscles are used in drive blocking or pass protection action as well as in any pushing or throwing action. The front of the deltoids work with the upper part of the chest muscle (the clavicular portion of the pectoralis major)

Photos 15.4a and 15.4b Incline fly

in this exercise. If the exercise is done flat on your back (the supine position), the pectorals will do more of the work. If you are on an incline with your head high, the deltoids will do more of the work.

Free weights (dumbbells) lend themselves well to this type of shoulder muscle isolation. Lie on your back on a flat or inclined bench with a dumbbell in each hand. Allow the weights to go out and down until they come at least to the level of your body, then raise them with slightly bent arms until your arms are vertical. This lateral raise is also called a fly (see photos 15.4a and 15.4b).

Abdominals

Most people are aware of how important it is to have abdominal strength. For one thing, it helps to keep our bellies tucked in for better posture. In addition, the abdominals help to stabilize the hips, which is essential for every athletic action that involves the hip joints—particularly in running and blocking. The abs also help support the low back, an area that many offensive linemen have a problem with.

To isolate your abdominals, lie on your back and bend your knees as much as possible so the muscles that flex the hip joint (bringing the thighs forward and upward) will not work as well. You should also keep your hips (your belt) on the mat when doing an abdominal exercise. Whenever your hips are pulled off the mat or bench, your hip flexors are working. (This is particularly harmful for people who have an excessive curvature in their lower backs. This curvature places a higher pressure on the outside of the discs in the lower back region and can cause many problems as a person grows older.)

Abdominal curl-ups are done by lying on the floor or on a bench with your knees bent and your hands on your chest or shoulders. (Some authorities believe that having the hands behind the head might increase the stress on the neck area, which is undesirable.) Curl your shoulders forward until your hips are about to leave the floor (see photo 15.5). Usually you will be able to touch your elbows to your thighs. A normal range of motion for abdominals is under 40 degrees. Keep your head up. Looking at the ceiling is a good idea. If you do the curl-ups on an inclined board with your head lower than your feet, you will increase the resistance you are lifting. If you are working for strength, you should hold weight plates on your chest in order to increase the resistance. But most people are looking for muscular endurance, to help hold their tummies in longer. If this is what you want, just do many repetitions.

Photo 15.5 Abdominal curl-up

In another exercise often done for the abdominals, the abdominal crunch, you lie flat on your back, then bring your knees and shoulders upward at the same time (see photo 15.6).

Side sit-ups are performed to strengthen the muscles on the side of the abdominal area (the obliques). Lie on your side and lift your shoulders from the mat or bench (see photo 15.7). For this exercise most people will have to have their feet

Photo 15.6 Abdominal crunch

Photo 15.7 Side sit-up on Roman chair

held down. (They can be hooked under a barbell or the bar of a Roman chair.) This exercise works not only the abdominal oblique muscles but also the muscles of your lower back and the rectus abdominis on the side to which you are bending. If you have access to a rotary abdominal machine you can do a twisting action that is designed to more effectively work the oblique muscles. You can also do a twisting sit-up. Bring the left shoulder upward first as you sit up. Return to the starting position and then bring the right shoulder up as you curl up.

Lower Back: Back Extensions and Dead Lift

Exercises for the lower back are probably the most important for the average person to do, because lower back injuries, especially muscle pulls, are so common. The lower back muscle are often neglected, however, possibly because they are less noticeable than many other muscles on our bodies. The lower back muscles are particularly important in weight lifting and football.

Back extensions can be done on the floor. Just lie face down and raise your shoulders and knees slightly off the floor. Current thinking is that the back should not be hyperextended (greatly arched).

In a gym there may be a Roman chair available. This will allow for a greater range of motion than the simple back extension. Put your hips on the small saddle, hook your feet under the bar, bend forward at the waist about 30 degrees, then straighten your back. If you desire strength, hold weight plates or a dumbbell behind your head. If you want muscular endurance, just do as many reps as you can (see photo 15.8).

The dead lift is a commonly used exercise for the lower back. The knees are slightly flexed. With the barbell on the floor (or preferably on blocks to reduce the strain on the knees and lower back), grip the bar with your palms toward your body. While keeping your back straight and head up, straighten up to the standing position (see photo 15.9).

The problem with this exercise is that it may place excess stress on the inside edges of the discs of the lower spine. The stress could weaken them. Also, the weight being lifted is at its maximum while the pressure on the discs is at its maximum. In addition, the amount of force your muscles are required to exert reduces during the exercise. By the time your back has moved through 30 degrees of motion, your muscles are lifting only 50 percent as much weight as they did when the weight was first being lifted from the floor. This can be a very dangerous lift if not done properly, and it is imperative that this lift be supervised by someone with knowledge of lifting. Young athletes should not attempt it.

Photo 15.8 Back extension with weight

Hip Flexors

The hip flexors bring the thighs forward, so they are essential in any running activity. If you strengthen the hip flexors and practice sprint-

Photo 15.9 Dead lift

ing you may be able to increase your stride frequency (number of strides per second) and decrease your sprint times. Hip flexors are exercised when the thigh is brought forward. This can be done several ways.

Using the lower pulley of a weight machine, hook your ankle into a handle or use an ankle strap to secure your ankle to the pulley (see photo 15.10). Raise your leg straight forward. This is the best exercise for punters and kickers. If a multi-hip machine is available, exercise through as full a range as possible with the resistance on your lower thigh, just above the knee (see photo 15.11).

While hanging from a high bar, bring your legs forward with your knees bent and touch your knees to your chest. Then bring your legs forward without bending your knees.

While standing, with or without weight boots, brace yourself with your arms and lift one leg forward as high as it will go. Bring it up slowly.

You can also use manual resistance to exercise the hip flexors. While lying on your side, have a partner give resistance against the leg or ankle as you move the leg forward.

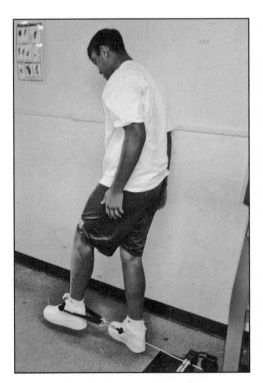

Photo 15.10 Hip flexor on low pulley

Photo 15.11 Hip flexor exercise on multi-hip machine

Knee Extensors: Leg Extensions

Extending the knee means straightening it. Knee extensors are used in any running, jumping, or competitive weight lifting activity. This action strengthens the whole quadriceps muscle (front of the thigh).

On the leg extension machine, hook your feet under the padded bar. Straighten your legs (see photo 15.12). This exercise can also be done with a weighted boot.

You can also exercise the knee extensors with a partner to provide resistance. Sit on a table and let your partner put both hands on your ankle (see photo 15.13). Straighten your leg while your partner gives you just enough resistance to allow you to make the movement.

Photo 15.12 Leg extension

Hip (Thigh) Extensors

The hip extensor muscles bring the thighs from a forward position back to a straight position (such as when you are standing). They will also bring the thighs farther back than straight. This is called *hyperextension*. The hip extensors are the muscles that supply power when you are running or jumping.

On a multi-hip machine, starting with your hip flexed, extend your thigh (see photo 15.14 on the next page). On a pulley machine with an ankle strap, face the machine and extend and hyperextend the thigh.

With a partner, lie on your back and bring your leg up. Let your partner stand and hold the back of your ankle, then resist as you lower your leg to the floor. Or, while

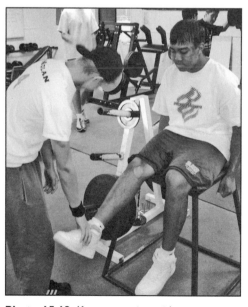

Photo 15.13 Knee extension with partner

standing, bracing yourself for balance, bring one leg backward as far as you can with your partner providing resistance. You can also do these exercises without a partner.

Knee Flexors: Leg Curls

The knee flexors bend the knee, decreasing the angle between the thigh and the lower leg. They work with the hip extensors and are important in running. It is also essential that if the fronts of the thighs (the quadriceps or knee extensors) are strengthened, the knee flexors (hamstrings) must also be strengthened. If the ratio of strength of the hamstrings is 60 percent or less that of the quadriceps, pulled muscles in the hamstring may result. The NFL recommendation is that the hamstrings be at least 75 percent as strong as the quadriceps.

On a leg extension machine, lie face down, hook your ankle under the bar, and flex your leg back at the knee joint. This exercise can also be done standing with a weighted boot.

With a partner, lie on the floor or a bench. Let your partner supply the resistance by putting his hands on the back of your ankle as you flex your knee joint (see photo 15.15).

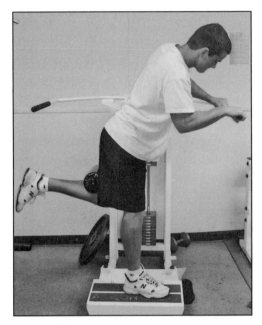

Photo 15.14 Backward hip (thigh) extension

Photo 15.15 Leg curl with partner

Knee and Hip Extensors: Squats, Leg Presses, and Lunges

The leg exercises we have described isolate one muscle action, but you play with all of these muscles working at the same time. It is therefore preferable to extend the hip, knee, and ankle joints at the same time. Squats, leg presses, and lunges utilize these full extensions. These are necessary for all running and blocking skills.

In performing a squat, make sure that the angle of your knee does not pass the 90-degree mark. At this point the ligaments that attach to the cartilages inside the knee are pulled back in the knee and act as fulcrums. The force of the weight downward on this fulcrum increases the stretch on the ligaments in the front of the knee and can stretch them—making the knee structurally weaker. If a person does a full squat, in which the muscles at the back of the thighs and the calf muscles touch, the fulcrum is moved farther to the rear, and great force is exerted on the ligaments in the front of the knee.

For maximum safety, squats must be done in the squat rack. In deciding how far down you will go in your squat, first determine why you want the strength. If you are a competitive weight lifter, you may wish to go past the 90-degree angle so that you can gain strength through a greater range of motion. But be aware that you may weaken the structure of your knee by stretching some of the ligaments. If you are a football lineman, you won't have to go past the 90-degree angle to develop the strength you need for your activity. In doing squats in the squat rack, be certain that the pins are set so that you cannot go too far down and damage your knees.

The most common positions for your feet are either shoulder width with the toes pointed straight ahead or a wider-than-shoulder position with the toes pointed slightly outward. The feet should remain flat through the entire lift (see photo 15.16).

Photo 15.16 Squat

Cautions: Be certain to keep your back slightly arched and your head level or up to reduce pressure on the spinal discs. Don't let your torso bend too far forward. Also don't let your knees get too far ahead of your toes. This would indicate that you are carrying too much weight forward, and you could lose your balance. It also increases the angle of the knee and can put harmful pressure on the ligaments. Furthermore, be careful not to bounce up from the squat position, because this too increases the strain on your knee ligaments. During the squatting action the bar should move up and down in a vertical path.

Two variations of the squat are the front squat, with the bar held on your chest, and the hack squat, with the bar held behind your back at the level of your buttocks.

On the leg press machine you have some built-in safety. By sitting down, you avoid the compressing force of the weight downward on your spinal discs. But the sitting posture is even further away from the playing posture (vertical or leaning forward) than is the squat. As in the squat rack, you can finish your leg press on the machine with a toe push (ankle plantar flexion) to make the exercise more like a jump or a sprinting stride.

Some gyms have sleds where you extend your legs, pushing upward with your shoulders at a forward angle. This is better for run blocking than the squat. But because the squat, leg press, and sled all use both feet at the same time, the previously mentioned Power Runner, in which you use your feet alternately, is preferred because the forward leaning posture and the alternate leg action more closely mimic the action of a blocking player.

If you don't have a full weight set and a squat rack and still want to do a squat exercise, you can do one-legged squats. Hold on to a table for balance, lift one foot off the floor, and squat with the other leg. This will give you the same effect as if you were carrying your body weight on a barbell. Another option is to stand on a wood box or bench and do the one-legged squat. This helps not only leg strength but balance also. For example, if you weigh 150 pounds and do a one-legged squat, that would be the same as doing a full squat holding a 150-pound barbell. This exercise is very valuable for people who are not consistent weight trainers but need good strength or muscular endurance for an event. It is a great preseason and in-season exercise for skiers.

Lunges work the same muscles as do squats. With a barbell held on your shoulders behind your neck (or dumbbells held at your sides), take a step forward and flex the forward leg as you settle into the lunge. Your knee should be no farther forward than your toes. Push yourself back up and bring the forward foot back to the starting position. You may need two smaller steps to safely return to the starting position.

Full-Body Extension: The Power Clean, Hang Clean, and Power Snatch

The power clean is essential for those wishing to develop full-body extension power. Football players fall into this category. The exercise works the knee and hip extensors, the ankle plantar flexors, the lower back, the deltoids, the upper trapezius, and the biceps. Other muscles are involved to a lesser extent. This is a great exercise because you start and end in a football position and use an explosive motion to move the weight, just as you explode into a defender.

The barbell should be on the floor close to your feet. With your feet about shoulder width apart, bend forward with your back slightly arched and grasp the bar with a wide grip and your palms facing toward you. Start the cleaning action with an explosive "jump" by straightening your hips, knees, and ankles while throwing your hips forward and up and pulling up with your shoulders in a shrugging motion. At the point where your legs are straightened the bar will be moving fast. Use this velocity to help you pull the bar to chest level (see photo 15.17). At the top of the movement, bring your wrists back and push the elbows forward and jump under the bar to allow the bar to settle on the top of your chest. At this point, flex your knees slightly to catch the weight. Then return the bar to the floor. This is a very technical lift that if done wrong can cause injury, and it must be supervised by someone with experience with this lift.

Another type of clean ends with the high pull, in which you lift the bar as high as possible, then return it to the floor without catching it.

Photo 15.17 Power clean

The hang clean is often used to teach the power clean. It can also be used for those with weak or injured knees or backs. In this exercise the barbell is dead-lifted to the tops of the knees. Then the clean motion is done from this position, throwing the hips forward and up and shrugging with the shoulders to raise the barbell to the clean position.

The power snatch starts like the clean, but the lifter pulls the bar above the shoulder level as high as possible. At the point where the bar is as high as it can be lifted, the lifter flexes the knees and locks the arms under the bar (see photo 15.18). This lift is done with a very wide grip and with lighter weights than the power clean. The most common mistakes are letting the bar move too far forward—away from the body—and letting the elbows drop just as one is completing the pull and making the "hop" under the bar. Do not do this exercise without knowledgeable supervision.

Photo 15.18 Power snatch

Calves: Calf Raises

Ankle plantar flexion occurs when the sole of your foot moves closer to your calf muscle, as when you rise up on your toes. This is a key area for strength and power in running and jumping, for diving, and for pushing off on a turn in swimming.

Holding a barbell on your shoulders, rise up on your toes. This is better done with the balls of your feet on a riser board or a large weight plate because your calf muscle will be gaining flexibility as you stretch down.

On a leg extension machine or sled machine, with your legs straight, allow the weight to bring your ankles back, stretching your Achilles tendon, then push the weight out with your calf muscles.

While holding a table or bar for balance, rise up on one toe (see photo 15.19). This will give you the same resistance as holding a barbell that equals your body weight and doing the exercise with two legs. For example, if you weigh 150 pounds and hold a barbell that weighs 150 pounds, each of your calf muscles will be lifting 150 pounds. If you hold no weight but do the exercise with only one leg, the calf muscle will still be lifting 150 pounds.

By holding a dumbbell in your free hand and doing the exercise with one leg at a time you get the same effect as adding double the amount to a barbell and doing the exercise with two legs.

Photo 15.19 Calf raise

Elbow (Triceps) Extension

The triceps are used to straighten the arms. They are therefore used in pushing something away from the body and in throwing. In football they are used for pass protection blocking and for hand shivers by defensive linemen; in weight lifting they help in the pressing action. Elbow extension is an absolutely essential strength need for offensive linemen. (Flexing the elbows is not a major factor for offensive linemen, so biceps curl exercises will not be listed here.)

The standing one-arm triceps extension is the best exercise for elbow extension. Start with the arm holding the dumbbell extended overhead. Steady that elbow with the other hand by holding just below the elbow on the extended arm. (This stops you from "cheating" by allowing other muscles to come into play.) Allow the dumbbell to lower as much as possible behind your arm. (This gives maximum flexibility.) Then raise the dumbbell overhead for strength.

To use your own muscles to give you resistance, flex one arm and put the hand of the other arm against the wrist of the flexed arm. Straighten the arm while resisting with the other hand.

Triceps, Shoulders, and Upper Chest: Bench Presses

The bench press is one of the most common exercises for offensive linemen. It is particularly valuable for pass protection strength. However, for football the bench press should not be done as the power lifters do it, with a wide grip, but rather with a narrow grip and with the elbows close to the body as they are when blocking.

The bench press works the triceps, the front of the shoulders, and the upper chest muscles. If any of these muscles are weak, the lifter should do exercises that isolate the weaker muscles and strengthen them along with working on the bench press.

Your back should remain on the bench throughout the exercise. If you arch you will be able to lift a bit more weight because more of your lower pectorals will come into play, but this is considered cheating.

Starting with the bar at arm's length and over your nose, slowly lower the bar to your chest, then push it upward. Be careful that you don't push it toward your feet or you might lose control of it. The proper path of the bar is an arc from a position over the lifter's nose, lowered to the area of the nipples, then lifted over the nose again. The bar should not go straight up from the chest, nor should it be bounced off the chest.

This exercise can be done with free weights using a rack and a spotter (see photos 15.20a and 15.20b) or without a rack using two spotters. The spotters are necessary to make certain that the lifter does not lose control of the weights and endanger himself. (Nearly all reported deaths related to strength training have occurred with boys doing bench presses alone and losing control of the weight, usually suffocating with the bar on the neck.)

The bench press can also be done on a machine. For offensive linemen this is better because the posture of the back is vertical—as it is when pass protecting. The brain is therefore stimulating the muscles in the correct posture. Another advantage of the machine is that it is safer. Also, on a machine your muscles do not have to balance the weights with other stabilizing muscles, since the balance is built into the machine. Some experts, however, argue that the

Photos 15.20a and 15.20b Narrow grip bench press with spotter

free weights force you to use other muscles than the primary muscles exercised, thereby stabilizing the joint. For example, in the bench press the primary movers are the chest and triceps muscles, but the deltoids, lats, and lower pectorals are all working to stabilize the lift so that the bar does not go too far toward your head or feet.

The incline bench press works the front (anterior) deltoids more than the upper chest. The angle of the incline press makes it more valuable for run blocking because of the upward lift used.

Dumbbells can also be pressed. The same muscles are also used in a push-up.

Hip Abduction/Adduction

As an offensive lineman you will have to move laterally as well as forward—particularly when pass protecting. Therefore hip abduction (moving the leg away from the center of the body) and hip adduction (bringing the leg back to the center of the body) are very important. The adduction exercises also help to prevent groin pulls.

On an abduction machine, just sit in the seat, hook your legs into the stirrups, and push both legs outward.

With a partner, lie on your back with your partner holding the outside of your feet or lower legs. Push your legs apart as far as they will go, with your partner resisting.

On a machine, use the lower pulley. While standing sideways to the machine at the low pulley station, hook your outer foot into the handle (or use an ankle strap) and pull your leg away from the machine.

Hip adduction exercises strengthen the muscles on the inside of the leg (the groin area). With an adduction machine, sit in the seat, put your legs on the proper part of the machine, and squeeze your legs together.

Photo 15.21 Hip adduction strengthening with a partner

With a partner, start with your legs spread and have your partner put his or her hands on the inside of your knees or lower legs and give you resistance as you squeeze your legs together (see photo 15.21).

On a machine with a low pulley, stand away from the machine, sideways to it with your inner foot in the ankle strap, and squeeze your leg in toward your body.

Exercises for Long Snappers

Long snappers should work on a low pulley for snapping strength (see photo 15.22). As an alternative they can use a lat machine and, while standing or kneeling, grip the cable with the arms straight and pull it straight down.

Weight Lifting Safety

Always practice safe procedures when weight lifting. Serious injuries or even death can result from weight lifting acci-

Photo 15.22 Exercise for snapping strength using a low pulley

dents. Use a rack if one is available for all heavy lifts, and always have a spotter when using free weights. The spotter should stand where he can best assist in controlling the weight. Usually this is behind the lifter. If no rack is available, use two spotters, one stationed at each end of the bar.

Checklist for Loading and Unloading a Barbell

Use the following procedure to safely load or unload a barbell:

1. Grip the weights firmly to avoid dropping them. (Loading and unloading the weights is a major cause of finger injury to lifters who don't use the proper loading techniques.)
2. When loading the bar, be certain that the hollow part of the weight is on the inside. This makes it easier to grip the plate. It is important that the weights on both sides of the bar match (hollow side in), or the bar will be off-balance.
3. Make certain that the bar is weighted correctly. If one side of the bar has heavier weights than the other, it will be significantly off-balance and can result in an accident and possible injury to the lifter.
4. Collars should always be used to keep the weight plates secure and to prevent them from sliding and unbalancing the bar.

$\boxed{16}$

Warming Up
and Conditioning
for Speed and Quickness

Most coaches have been taught to warm up their athletes by doing a number of stretches and some movement exercises such as running. It was believed that stretching made the muscles more ready to contract, reduced delayed onset muscle soreness (DOMS), and reduced the chance for muscle injuries. There was no scientific evidence for these beliefs—only tradition. Sport research has now shown this to be completely wrong. An analysis of studies in the area shows that stretching alone generally does not prevent injuries. In some cases it increases injuries. A number of studies indicate that:

- The muscles do not function as well after stretching because the stiffness required for maximal force is reduced by the stretching. Stretching as a part of the warm-up reduces power by 4 to 8 percent.
- Stretching before an exercise will have no positive effect on a muscle that will not be required to elongate during the activity, such as jogging or running.
- Stretching doesn't increase the compliance (effective action) of a muscle during eccentric (lengthening) contractions. These lengthening

153

contractions are the sort of contractions most often associated with muscle and tendon injury.

- Most muscle injuries occur in the normal range of motion, not in a lengthened state, so stretching will not reduce the causative factors.
- Muscle and connective tissue injuries are generally higher among those who stretch.
- Stretching can produce damage to muscles and tendons at the cellular level.
- Stretching seems to mask muscular pain in humans. This seems to be why stretching an injured muscle or tendon may make it feel better even though additional damage may be occurring.
- Delayed onset muscle soreness does not seem to be reduced by stretching or massage.

Perhaps as many as 10 percent of athletes may need to stretch because the muscle cells that contract, called *sarcomeres*, may be so tight that there is no room to contract more (see fig. 16.1). This condition is called *contractures*. Also, the prohibition against stretching does not apply to stretching for increased flexibility—which, if needed, should be done after practice when the muscles are thoroughly warmed up.

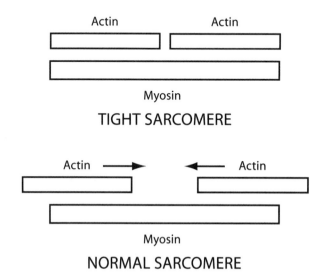

Figure 16.1 The microscopic elements of the muscle fiber where muscle contraction occurs

I am often asked what a young athlete can do to become a better football player. I always say that the more sports a person plays, the better he or she will be in all of them. I took something out of every sport I played while growing up. I was all conference in three sports in high school, and each of them helped me on my way to the pros.

I was a catcher in baseball. This gave me great leg and butt strength from being in the crouch all the time. I also learned hand-eye coordination to help time the punches on pass protection. Basketball is one of the best sports a young offensive lineman can play. Basically, offensive line play is just like playing defense in basketball, except you can use your hands.

Wrestling, in which many big offensive lineman participate, teaches leverage and timing. Track, especially the throws, teaches technique and explosion.

I was lucky in that the high school I attended wasn't big enough that I had to decide on only one sport when I was younger. If I had had to make a choice, I would have chosen basketball because I was a much better high school basketball player than football player, but I had much more potential in football.

Warming up Effectively

There is basic scientific evidence to suggest that an active warm-up may be protective against muscle strain injury. Warming the muscles should be done by slowly doing your sport-specific movements. Footwork drills, pass protection movements, pulling, and so forth are the types of activities that will effectively warm up your muscles and get your heart ready to perform.

There are other nonsport and nonlifting things that can be done to help players become stronger and more agile. Three of my favorites are dots, form running, and plyometrics.

Dots—for Quick Feet

Dots are a great way to improve foot speed and balance, and the setup is simple. All you need to do is spray paint five dots on the pavement for each station.

Four dots should form a square with eighteen inches between them on the sides of the square. The fifth dot should be in the middle of the square (similar to the "five" on dice). The players will do a series of moves with their feet using the dots as aiming points.

The first drill starts with the player's feet on the two dots at the bottom of the box. On the command to go, the player jumps his right foot to the middle dot, then both feet to the top dots, then the right foot to the middle dot again, and then both feet to the bottom dots. Keep repeating this for a period of fifteen to twenty seconds. Have another player do the same thing while the first rests. The first player then repeats the drill, except that he puts the left foot on the middle dot. Alternate again. Then do the drill putting both feet on the middle dot. Next, the player puts the right foot in the middle, but when he gets to the top two dots, he spins around and faces the other way, then puts the right foot in the middle and both feet on the far dots and spins again. Then do this putting the left foot in the middle. Don't do this one too long or the players will get sick from spinning.

For the next drill, start with both feet on the lower right dot. At the command, have the player jump with both feet together to the middle dot, then the upper left dot, across to the upper right dot, back to the middle dot, to the lower left dot, and back to the lower right dot. This will form a Z pattern. After alternating, start at the lower left dot and go opposite from the proceeding drill in a backward Z.

Make a game out of this drill. See who can get the most reps in during the time period. Keep a chart of how the players are progressing. While this drill is tiring, it can also be made fun and challenging.

Form Running

Form running is not as easy as it sounds. Most kids do not know how to run properly. They just start running when they are little and never work on the correct way to do it. You may say that offensive linemen don't have to know how to run because they do not often have to run far, but form running will help improve their speed and coordination.

Form running is done at a very slow pace so that you emphasize the motion and can show that it is being done correctly. You want to mimic the form used by sprinters. The arms are very important. The hands should be held open like a knife to cut the air. They should be turned in so they face each other and kept just wider than the body. The elbows should be kept close to the body. The hands should come up as high as the shoulder and come down to the hip pocket on the downswing. The arms will work opposite from the feet, meaning that when the right foot and knee come up, the left hand will come up, and vice versa. The knees should be brought up as high as possible while keeping an upright upper body. The toes should be pointed forward at all times. This is an area where many players have a problem. The pace should be very slow so that the players can get the feel of the coordinated movement between the arms and legs. As they progress, have them do the form running a little faster. As the speed increases, the body lean will have to go forward slightly.

Coaches should make sure that when the players are doing their conditioning running, they do it using good form. This will help them run faster and build good techniques.

Plyometrics

Plyometrics is a fancy way of saying training through jumping. Jumping helps build the fast-twitch muscles and also works on explosive strength. Here is a series of drills that can be done with no equipment and also a few that need very basic types of equipment.

The first drill is to have the players start on the goal line and jump, using two feet, as far out as they can, stop and regroup themselves, and then continue jumping until they go twenty yards. The fewer jumps they need the better. The next drill is to do the same thing, only do not stop and regroup after each jump but go for speed for twenty yards. The players can use their upper bodies to get momentum working for them. This will also build coordination.

The next drill is jumping from one foot and landing on the other with no stopping for twenty yards. Once again, use the upper body for explosion and balance. The last drill is jumping off one foot and landing on the same foot, continuing for ten yards without stopping. Then repeat using the other foot.

The following drills take some very basic equipment. Build five wood boxes of heights from one foot to three feet, with each box six inches higher than the last. Using the one-foot box, have the players jump onto and off the box continuously without stopping for thirty seconds. See how many times they can do this in the time period. Once again, to make it fun, keep track of how many each gets and make a game out of it. Repeat using just one foot, then the other foot. As the players get better, use the eighteen-inch box, then the twenty-four-inch box if they can do it without risk of injury.

The higher boxes should be used for single jumps where the players jump up, come back down, then jump again. The less time you spend on the ground between jumps the more effective the exercise. So get off the ground immediately. The height of the box used should be determined by the ability of the player to make the jump. As players get proficient on one box, have them move on to the next.

Plyometrics can also be used for arm strength and quickness. Two players assume their pass protection stances. They can start four to six feet apart, eventually increasing that distance. Take a medicine ball of a weight the players can manage and toss it back and forth as quickly as possible. The players should not catch the ball and recoil to throw it, but rather catch and throw the ball in a continuous motion. The arms should react as if in pass protection—with the hands moving only six to eight inches in the catch-throw reaction.

17

Nutrition and Hydration for the Offensive Line

O ur ability to become better conditioned is limited if we do not get sufficient amounts of the essential nutrients. This chapter on general nutrition will also point out some of the relationships between food and exercise. This should give you a more complete picture of this area of conditioning.

A basic understanding of the science of nutrition is essential to healthy living. An informed person will be aware of the nutrients necessary for minimal and optimal functioning, then put that knowledge into practice by developing a proper diet. Unfortunately, very few people consume even the minimum amounts of all of the necessary nutrients—protein, fat, carbohydrates, vitamins, minerals, and water (the essential nonnutrient). The first three nutrients listed (protein, fat, and carbohydrates) bring with them the energy required to keep us alive, in addition to other specific contributions to our bodies.

The calorie used in counting food energy is really a kilocalorie, one thousand times larger than the calorie used as a measurement of heat in chemistry class. In one food calorie (kilocalorie), there is enough energy to heat one kilogram of water 1°C (or 2.2 pounds 1.8°F), or to lift three thousand pounds of weight one foot high. So those little calories you see listed on the cookie packages pack a lot of energy.

Most people need about 10 calories per pound of body weight per day just to stay alive. If you plan to do something other than just lie in bed all day, you may need about 17 calories per pound to keep yourself going. Most athletes, particularly endurance athletes, need much more.

You can roughly figure your caloric needs using the following numbers. (These figures are for recreational athletes, not top-level athletes.) Football players use about 1.67 calories per pound per hour. Therefore, a two-hundred-pound lineman would use about 335 calories per hour.

Protein

Protein is made up of twenty-two amino acids. These are made up of carbon, hydrogen, oxygen, and nitrogen. While both fats and carbohydrates also contain the first three elements, nitrogen is found only in protein. Protein is essential for building nearly every part of the body—the brain, heart, organs, skin, muscles, and even the blood. Since offensive linemen need a great deal of muscle tissue it is essential to take in enough protein.

There are four calories in one gram of protein. Strength athletes require about 1.2 to 1.4 grams of protein per kilogram of body weight per day. This translates into about one-half gram of protein per pound. So, an easy estimate for your protein requirements in grams per day would be to divide your body weight by 3. For instance, if you weigh 150 pounds, you need about 50 grams of protein per day.

Physically active adults have been thought to require more protein than is recommended by the United States recommended daily allowance (USRDA), which is set at 0.8 grams per kilogram of body weight per day; 1.2 to 1.4 is recommended for football players. Most active people need not eat additional protein if they consume 12 to 15 percent of their total calories as protein. Excess protein consumption (above the body's requirement) will be broken down and the calories will either be burned off or stored as fat.

The purpose of strength training is to build muscle, and you don't want to do anything to hamper this process. Therefore, those who participate in heavy resistance training may choose to follow a diet higher in protein (1.2 to 1.4 grams per kilogram per day) to elicit maximum benefits from their workout.

In order to make any body part, including muscle, you must first have all of the necessary amino acids. Some of them your body can manufacture, while others you must get from your food. Those amino acids that you must get from your food are called the essential amino acids, while the others that you can make are known as the nonessential amino acids. During childhood, nine of the twenty-two amino acids are essential, but in adulthood we acquire the ability to synthesize one additional amino acid, leaving us with eight essential amino acids that we must get from food.

Amino acids cannot be stored in the body. Therefore, athletes need to consume an adequate amount of protein every day. If adequate protein is not consumed, the body immediately begins to break down tissue (usually beginning with muscle tissue) to release the essential amino acids. If even one essential amino acid is lacking, the other essential ones are not able to work to their full capacities. For example, if methionine (the most commonly lacking amino acid) is present at 60 percent of the minimum requirement, the other seven essential amino acids are limited to near 60 percent of their potential. When they are not used, amino acids are deaminated and excreted as urea in the urine.

Animal products (such as fish, poultry, and beef) and animal by-products (milk, eggs, cheese) are rich in readily usable protein. These sources have all of the essential amino acids in them and therefore can be converted into the needed protein in your body. These foods are called complete protein sources.

Incomplete protein sources are any other food sources that provide protein but not high levels of all of the essential amino acids. Some examples of incomplete proteins include beans, peas, and nuts. These food sources must be combined with other food sources, called complementary foods, that have the missing essential amino acids so that you can make protein in your body. Some examples of complementary foods are rice and beans, or peanut butter on whole wheat bread.

Another reason to be aware of specific food combinations is to enhance the absorption of the protein consumed. The person who is aware of the varying qualities of proteins can combine protein sources to take advantage of the strengths of each. For example, if a piece of toast or coffee cake is eaten at breakfast and washed down with coffee, and then a glass of milk is consumed at lunch, each of the protein sources would be absorbed by the body at a lower potential. But if the bread was consumed with the milk at either meal, the needed complementary amino acids would be available and higher protein values of both would be absorbed by the body.

Protein supplements are often used by weight trainers and athletes. These supplements may not be a good value because they usually fall far short of an

The essential amino acids and some foods containing them:

- Isoleucine: fish, beef, organ meats, eggs, shellfish, whole wheat, soybeans, milk
- Leucine: beef, fish, organ meats, eggs, soybeans, shellfish, whole wheat, milk, liver
- Lysine: fish, beef, organ meats, shellfish, eggs, soybeans, milk, liver
- Methionine: fish, beef, shellfish, egg whites, milk, liver, whole wheat, cheese
- Phenylalanine: beef, fish, egg whites, whole wheat, shellfish, organ meats, soybeans, milk
- Threonine: fish, beef, organ meats, eggs, shellfish, soybeans, liver
- Tryptophan: soy milk, fish, beef, soy flour, organ meats, shellfish, egg whites
- Valine: beef, fish, organ meats, eggs, soybeans, milk, whole wheat, liver

effective balance of the essential amino acids. While six of the essential amino acids are usually present in good quantities in these supplements, methionine and tryptophan are usually found in lesser amounts—and they are the most commonly lacking of the amino acids. Since 6 grams per pound of methionine (13 milligrams per kilogram) and 1.6 grams of tryptophan (3.5 grams per kilogram) per day are the recommended daily allowances, you might check to determine how much of these are actually contained in a supplement. This is especially important if your diet is lacking in either one or both of these amino acids and you are relying on the supplement to account for your protein needs. A better and cheaper source of protein for one needing a supplement would be powdered milk. If your diet is deficient in protein, you might also consider using egg whites (or egg substitutes), milk, or chicken. These may prove less expensive and more nutritious than the protein supplement.

Fats

Fat is made of carbon, hydrogen, and oxygen. There are nine calories in a gram of fat. In the body, fat is used to develop the myelin sheath that surrounds the nerves. It also aids in the absorption of vitamins A, D, E, and K, which are the fat-soluble vitamins. It serves as a protective layer around our vital organs, and it is a good insulator against the cold. It is also a highly concentrated energy source. And, of course, its most redeeming quality is that it adds flavor and juiciness to food!

Just as protein is broken down into different kinds of nitrogen compounds called amino acids, there are also different kinds of fats. The three major kinds of fats (also called fatty acids) are saturated fats, monounsaturated fats, and polyunsaturated fats. A more newly recognized type of fat is trans-fatty acids, which are created when unsaturated fats are converted to a harder saturated-like fat in foods through hydrogenation. This occurs when oils, such as corn and safflower, are hardened to make margarines and other products.

Saturated fats are "saturated" with hydrogen atoms. They are generally solid at room temperature and are generally found in animal fats, egg yolks, and whole milk products. Since these are the fats that are primarily responsible for raising blood cholesterol level and hardening the arteries, they should be minimized. Because linemen are generally larger people and more prone to heart disease and being overweight, it is important that linemen be aware of effective nutrition and diet, especially when they finish their athletic careers.

Monounsaturated fats (oleic fatty acids) have room for two hydrogen ions to double bond to one carbon. They are liquid at room temperature. Dietary monounsaturated fats have been shown to have the greatest effect on the reduction of cholesterols, particularly the harmful LDLs, thereby contributing a positive effect on atherosclerosis. The best sources of these are canola (rapeseed) oil and olive oil. Many nuts also contain high amounts of monounsaturates.

Polyunsaturated fats (linoleic fatty acids) have at least two carbon double bonds available, which translates into space for at least four hydrogen ions. Polyunsaturated fats are also liquid at room temperature and are found in the highest proportions in vegetable sources. Safflower, corn, and linseed oils are good sources of this type of fat. Polyunsaturated fatty acids of the omega-3 type, found primarily in fatty fish (especially salmon, trout, and herring) may also contribute to the prevention of atherosclerosis.

Carbohydrates

Carbohydrates are made from carbon, hydrogen, and oxygen, just as are fats, but "carbs" are generally a simpler type of molecule. There are four calories in a gram of carbohydrate. If not utilized immediately for energy as sugar (glucose), they are either stored in the body as glycogen (the stored form of glucose) or synthesized into fat and stored. Of the digestible carbohydrates, there are two categories: simple and complex. Simple carbohydrates are the most readily usable energy source in the body and include such things as sugar, honey, and fruit. Complex carbohydrates are the starches. Complex carbs also break down into sugar for energy, but their breakdown is slower than that of simple carbs. Also, complex carbohydrates such as whole grains, fruits, and vegetables bring with them various vitamins, minerals, and fiber. Since muscles use carbohydrates for fuel, linemen who work with strength training or work out hard need carbohydrates for energy. Of course, if the lineman is overweight the fats and carbohydrates can be reduced to get one's weight under control.

People in the United States often eat too many simple carbohydrates. These are the so-called "empty calories." They are empty because they have no vitamins, minerals, or fiber. While a person who uses a great deal of energy can consume these empty calories without weight gain, most of us find these empty calories settling on our hips. The average person consumes 125 pounds of sugar per year, which is equivalent to one teaspoon every forty minutes, night and day. Since each teaspoon of sugar contains 17 calories, this amounts to 231,000 calories or sixty-six pounds of potential body fat if this energy is not used as fuel for daily living.

High carbohydrate diets that are especially high in sugar may be hazardous to your health. They can increase the amount of triglycerides produced in the liver. Triglycerides are blood fats and are possible developers of hardened arteries. Also, a diet high in simple carbohydrates can lead to obesity, which may then result in the development of type 2 diabetes. But if your exercise regime uses a great many calories each day the triglycerides will be reduced. This will then reduce the "bad" low-density lipoprotein (LDL) or cholesterol and thereby increase the ratio of the good high-density lipoprotein (HDL).

Vitamins

Vitamins are organic compounds that are essential in small amounts for the growth and development of animals and humans. They act as enzymes (catalysts) that facilitate many of the body processes. Although there is some controversy as to the importance of consuming excess vitamins, it is acknowledged that we need a minimum amount of vitamins for proper functioning. Now that the role of certain vitamins in reducing the destructive impact of free oxygen radicals has been established, it is generally recommended that these vitamins be included in the daily intake at higher levels than were earlier recommended.

Some vitamins are soluble only in water; others need fat to be absorbed by the body. The water-soluble vitamins, the B complex and vitamin C, are more fragile than the fat-soluble vitamins. This is because they are more easily destroyed by the heat of cooking and if boiled, they lose a little of their potency into the water. Since they are not stored by the body, they should be included in the daily diet.

The fat-soluble vitamins, A, D, E, and K, need oils in the intestines to be absorbed by the body. They are more stable than the water-soluble vitamins and are not destroyed by normal cooking methods. Because they are stored in the body, there is the possibility of ingesting too much of them—especially vitamins A and D.

Nutritional researchers disagree as to whether vitamin supplements are necessary. But they are generally in agreement that natural vitamins are no better than synthetically prepared vitamins. Thus, synthetically made ascorbic acid is the same as the vitamin C found in strawberries, for example.

Free oxygen radicals are single atoms of oxygen that can combine with many molecules and tissues. They are harmful substances produced by many natural body processes. Physical exercise, for all of its benefits, is one producer of free oxygen radicals. So is smoking and air pollution. In fact just the normal processes of living, even sleeping, produce some free oxygen radicals. It is estimated that between 3 and 15 percent of all oxygen (O_2) goes through a stage where it is a free oxygen radical. Since free oxygen radicals have been implicated in starting some cancers and heart disease, it is wise for anyone, especially those who exercise, to take supplements that reduce these dangerous atoms. The antioxidants most commonly used are beta carotene (a vegetable precursor to vitamin A), vitamins C and E, selenium, and coenzyme Q10.

A normal multivitamin and mineral pill should be enough to supply your daily needs, but a few other supplements might help. Taking a B complex capsule may aid in utilizing your protein and carbohydrate intakes since some B vitamins aid in breaking down proteins and others in breaking down carbs. Many of the antioxidants can be found in one pill. Other supplements to consider might be oat bran, rice bran, apple pectin, and other soluble fibers that can aid in getting rid of cholesterol as they pass through the intestines. Since larger people, including linemen, are more likely to have heart problems as they get older, it may be wise to reduce the harmful cholesterol throughout life rather than waiting until there are artery problems in your forties and fifties.

Minerals

Minerals form structural components of the body, and they also participate in certain body processes. The body uses many minerals—phosphorus, calcium, and magnesium for strong teeth and bones; zinc for growth; chromium for carbohydrate metabolism; and copper and iron for hemoglobin production in the blood.

Iron is used primarily in developing hemoglobin, which carries the oxygen in the red blood cells. Most boys and men get sufficient iron in their diets.

Magnesium is the eighth most abundant element on the earth's surface. It seems to help activate enzymes essential to energy transfer. It is crucial for effective contraction of the muscles. Exercise depletes this element, so supplementation may be called for. When magnesium is not present in sufficient amounts, twitching, tremors, and undue anxiety may develop.

Calcium is primarily responsible for the building of strong bones and teeth. For this reason, it seems obvious that a diet chronically low in calcium would have a negative effect on one's bone strength. Calcium is also necessary for nerve transmission, blood clotting, and muscle contractions. Without enough calcium, muscle cramps often result.

Potassium is a chief mineral in cell growth. A deficiency can cause impaired nerve and muscle function ranging from paralysis to minor weakness, loss of appetite, nausea, depression, apathy, drowsiness, confusion, heart failure, and even death. Potassium also helps to regulate the acid/base balance of the blood and to regulate blood pressure.

Sodium, along with potassium, helps to maintain the body's water balance. But too much sodium can raise blood pressure in some people because too much water is retained. Because sodium is the major mineral ingredient in sweat it occasionally needs to be increased in very hot weather or when an athlete perspires a lot.

Chromium helps to regulate blood sugar and to metabolize fats and carbohydrates. It is also an antioxidant.

Selenium is a mineral that is part of an essential enzyme, glutathione peroxidase, that protects the naturally occurring antioxidant glutathione. Selenium works with vitamins C, E, and beta carotene. It may, as vitamin E, reduce microinjuries to the small muscle fibers. It may also reduce the risk of digestive cancers, especially of the stomach and esophagus. In fact, selenium seems to be protective against all cancers.

Weight Control

While linemen are usually encouraged to gain weight, many put on too much fat. The fat not only slows down their reactions but also makes them fatigue more easily. In a recent conversation with Tom Flores, former Oakland Raider Super Bowl coach, he commented that the Denver Broncos were the best zone blocking team in the NFL because they were leaner and quicker. "Most teams just have a bunch of fat guys trying to block." So keeping your body fat percentage down should make you a quicker and more agile blocker. Technique is much more important than weight.

Sensible eating requires understanding of the basic principles of nutrition. The nutrients must appear in the diet in proper quantities, and the calories must be the amount necessary to maintain one's sports activities and desired weight. Caloric needs change according to climate and the amount of activity in which a person participates. It is obvious that hot weather necessitates a greater intake of fluids due to the loss of water through perspiration. There is also a lesser need for calories because the body does not need to burn as many calories to maintain its 98.6°F temperature.

Important Considerations in Selecting Your Diet

The Federal Department of Agriculture has devised a suggested diet guide called the food pyramid. There are six food groups in the pyramid:

- Grain products (breads, cereals, pastas): 6 to 11 servings per day recommended
- Vegetables: 3 to 5 servings per day
- Fruits: 2 to 4 servings per day
- High-protein meats and meat substitutes (meat, poultry, fish, beans, nuts, eggs): 2 to 3 servings per day

- Milk products: 2 servings for adults, 3 for children
- Extra calories, if needed, from fats and/or sweets

Grain products give the carbohydrates needed for energy. A serving size would be one slice of bread, an ounce of dry cereal, or a half cup of cooked cereal, pasta, or rice.

The grains are rich in B vitamins, some minerals, and fiber. Whole grains are the best sources of fiber. Refining grains or polishing rice reduces the fiber, the mineral content, and the B vitamins. This occurs in white and "wheat" bread (which is often not whole wheat, but rather white bread with brown coloring added), pastas, pastries, and white rice. The flour in these products is often refortified with three of the B-complex vitamins, but seldom with the other essential nutrients contained in whole grain products.

Vegetables are rich in fiber, beta carotene, and some vitamins and minerals. If you are trying to lose weight, many vegetables can be helpful because they are high in water and in fiber, and thus filling but low in calories. Among these are all greens (including lettuce, cabbage, and celery) as well as cauliflower. Actually, most vegetables are quite low in calories. A serving size would be a half cup of raw or cooked vegetables or a cup of raw leafy vegetables.

Fruits are generally high in vitamin C and fiber. They are also relatively low in calories. A serving size would be a quarter cup of dried fruit, a half cup of cooked fruit, three-quarters cup of fruit juice, a whole piece of fruit, or a wedge of a melon.

Protein sources such as meats, eggs, nuts, and beans are high in minerals and vitamins B_6 and B_{12}. A serving would be two-and-a-half ounces of cooked meat, poultry, or fish, two egg whites, four tablespoons of peanut butter, or one-and-a-quarter cups of cooked beans. A MacDonald's Quarter Pounder would give you two servings. The hidden eggs in cakes and cookies also count. The best meat products to eat are egg whites and poultry without the skin.

Red meat not only has a relatively low quality of protein (after egg whites, milk, fish, poultry, and organ meats), but it is linked to both cancers and heart disease. It also carries a great amount of fat, even if the fat on the outside is trimmed off. There is also a great deal of cholesterol in the meat and fat of all land animals.

Of the "flesh" proteins, fish is the best. It is a higher quality of protein than meat or poultry, and it contains the helpful omega-3 oils. Fish are able to convert the polyunsaturated linolenic fatty acid from plants that they eat into omega-3 oils. These work to prevent heart disease by reducing cholesterol and by making the blood less likely to clot in the arteries. They do this by interfering with the production of the prostaglandin thromboxane, which increases blood clotting.

Milk and milk products (cheeses, yogurt, ice cream) are high in calcium and protein as well as some minerals (potassium and zinc) and riboflavin. A serving would be one cup of milk or yogurt, one-and-a-half ounces of cheese, two cups of cottage cheese, one-and-a-half cups of ice cream, or one cup of pudding or custard. Adults need two servings daily, children need three.

Fats and sweets should be consumed only if a person needs extra calories. Fats over the recommended maximum of 30 percent of one's diet can be quite harmful—particularly in causing cancers and hardened arteries. Most researchers suggest a maximum of 10 to 20 percent of calories in fats, most in the form of monounsaturated and polyunsaturated fatty acids.

For a Healthier Diet

Avoid milk fat by drinking nonfat milk and milk products, eating ice milk (3 percent fat), frozen no-fat yogurt or frozen desserts made without milk fat, and eating nonfat or low fat cheeses. Half of the calories in whole milk come from the 3.5 percent of fat in the milk. Low fat (2 percent) milk has reduced the fat calories by 40 percent. When low fat milk is advertised as 98 percent fat free, it is not that much better than whole milk, which is 96.5 percent fat free. Most of milk is water. The fats in milk are highly saturated—the worst kind of fat. Yet the protein quality of milk is very high.

Egg yolks should be avoided because they contain a great deal of cholesterol and saturated fat. They are second only to caviar (fish eggs) in cholesterol content. Egg whites, however, have the highest rating for protein quality.

Reduce fats to between 10 and 20 percent of your calories if you are concerned about heart problems. (U.S. guidelines suggest no more than 30 percent.) Use fat-free salad dressing or vinegar or lemon juice only. Rather than butter or margarine, buy whole grain bread and eat it without spread. If you must use spread use olive oil, or perhaps olive oil and garlic as they serve in many Italian restaurants. Or, if calories are not a concern and you like sweets, use a jelly or jam.

Never fry foods in oil, use a nonstick pan. If you must have an oil use canola, olive, or safflower oil. Stay away from all fried foods, including potato chips. Fried foods not only add calories and saturated fats, but they increase your chances for intestinal cancers—as do all fats.

Beverages

Beverages make up a large part of our diets. We often don't think much about the kinds of liquids we drink. Drinks have been rated by the Center for Science in the Public Interest according to the amount of fat and sugar (higher content results in a lower rating) and the amount of protein, vitamins, and minerals (higher content results in a higher rating). Skim or nonfat milk was rated +47, whole milk +38 (the lower rating was because of its fat content), orange juice +33, Hi-C +4, coffee 0, coffee with sugar −12, Kool-Aid −55, and soft drinks −92.

Milk is the best beverage for most people. Linemen should drink a good deal of skim or nonfat milk. In addition to its nutrient value as a developer of bones and organs, milk has been found to help people sleep. They go to sleep more quickly, then sleep longer and more soundly. This is because of milk's high content of the amino acid tryptophan, which makes serotonin, the neurotransmitter associated with relaxation and calming activity.

Coffee contains several ingredients that may be harmful to the body, including stimulants such as caffeine and the xanthines, oils that seem to stimulate the secretion of excess acid in the stomach, and diuretics that eliminate water and some nutrients, such as calcium, from the body. Even two cups of coffee a day increases the risk of bone fractures.

Alcohol contains seven calories per gram. These calories contain no nutritional elements, but they do contribute to your total caloric intake. Since alcoholic drinks are surprisingly high in calories, they greatly contribute to the weight problems of many individuals. Alcohol is also a central nervous system depressant that causes a decrease in one's metabolism. This is, of course, a major negative for football players.

How to Lose Weight

The wisest approach to losing weight would be to find out why you are overweight. If it is genetic, perhaps medical help is needed. If you eat because of stress, you could find another method to relieve the stress, such as exercise or relaxation techniques or, if you must have something in your mouth, you could try gum or a low-calorie food.

To make weight loss permanent, you must have a plan that will give you a lifelong change of habits. You will have to make certain that you have the proper amount of protein (about half of a gram for every pound of body weight), your fat consumption should be low (10 to 20 of total calories), and you should have an array of complex carbohydrates to give you the vitamins, minerals, and fiber you need.

To aid in your pursuit of weight loss, you may decide to change your eating habits. It is a good idea to eat smaller, more frequent meals rather than infrequent, large meals. Every time you eat, you increase your metabolism because you put your digestive system to work. There is evidence that eating four or five small meals a day is better than eating two or three large ones. It also seems to reduce the cholesterol level of the blood.

Another approach to dieting is to eliminate some foods at some meals—instead of having potatoes every night, have them every other night. Or you may decide to have open-faced sandwiches instead of sandwiches with two slices of bread. (Some people use lettuce leaves instead of bread to make a sandwich.) Switching from red meat to poultry or fish and from regular ice cream to a light version can save you calories while maintaining your nutritional status.

To lose one pound of fat per week, you must have a net deficit of 500 calories per day because one pound of fat contains 3,500 calories. You may choose to achieve this solely by decreasing your food intake by 500 calories per day. However, if this is your approach, be warned: your metabolism will slowly decrease over time to accommodate for the decrease in food energy, thereby making it harder and harder for you to continue to lose fat. Therefore, you should exercise as you reduce calories.

Water and Hydration

We walk, run, play, or compete in nearly all temperatures. Because of this we must be aware of the dangers of being too hot or too cold. We must also recognize the importance of replacing our body fluids before, during, and after our workouts. In earlier days football players were not allowed water during practices. Luckily those days have changed. Most deaths in football are related to overheating, not blocking or tackling.

When Cory Stringer of the Vikings died from heat-related causes it made coaches and players more aware of the problems of heat exhaustion and dehydration.

The Body's Cooling Systems

Excess heat not only negatively affects our performance but it also can be a source of serious health problems. As the outside temperature increases it becomes less and less possible to get rid of the body heat exercise produces. For example, if exercising at 37°F (3°C) you are 20 percent more effective in eliminating body heat than if you are exercising at 67°F (20°C) and 150 percent more effective than if you were exercising at 104°F (40°C). It is not uncommon for the body to reach a temperature of 104 to 106°F (40 to 41°C) when exercising. But normal resting body temperature is 98.6°F (37°C). The high heat makes it difficult, or impossible, for the perspiration to evaporate, so the body can't be effectively cooled.

The heat generated in the muscles is released by:

- Conduction—from the warmer muscles to the cooler skin
- Convection—heat loss from the skin to the air
- Evaporation—perspiration being vaporized

Conduction occurs through the body's liquids, such as the blood, absorbing the heat created by the contraction of the muscles and moving it to the cooler skin. Water can absorb many thousand times more heat than can the air, so it is an excellent conductor of heat from the muscles.

Convection occurs when the heat near the skin is absorbed into the atmosphere. For a swimmer in a cool pool, effective convection is very easy. For the runner it is more difficult. Because of the number of pads worn by football players there is less skin exposed to the air or to cloth. Helmets and shoulder, hip, thigh, knee, rib, and arm pads eliminate the possibility of getting the heat in the skin to the air. Convection is aided by a lower air temperature and by wind. A four-mile-an-hour wind is twice as effective in cooling as is a one-mile-an-hour wind. (This is the basis for the windchill factor associated with winds in cool environments.)

Evaporation is the most effective method for cooling the body that is exercising in the air. Each liter of sweat that evaporates takes with it 580 kilocalories. This is enough heat to raise the temperature of ten liters of water 58°C (10.5 quarts of water 105°F). This amounts to a cooling effect of over a half a kilocalorie per gram of perspiration evaporated. The evaporation of the sweat produces the cooling effect as the perspiration goes from liquid to gas. As the skin is cooled by the evaporation of the sweat, the skin is able to take more of the heat from the blood and thereby cool the blood so that it can pick up more heat from the muscles.

Humidity is the most important factor regulating the evaporation of sweat. High humidity reduces the ability of perspiration to be evaporated. It also is restricted by the pads worn. Exercising in a rubber suit has similar effects to high humidity because the sweat cannot evaporate—so it is not recommended.

Wind has the opposite effect. It affects the body temperature by cooling it faster than the air temperature alone. This is the windchill factor reported in the weather forecast on cold days. But even on warmer days the wind will evaporate the perspiration and cool the body faster than might otherwise be expected. This may increase the need for fluids to continue the production of sweat.

Fluid, Electrolyte, and Carbohydrate Replacement

The hyperthermia (high temperature) developed during exercise, particularly when the sweat cannot evaporate, is a major cause of fatigue. This is particularly true when the body has lost 2 percent of its water through perspiration. Since it is not uncommon to lose one to five liters of water when exercising, it is not difficult to enter the stage of dehydration. The combination of dehydration and high body temperature can cause a number of physiological problems such as a reduction of blood volume, an increase in the breakdown of liver and muscle glycogen (a sugar used for muscle energy), and the inability of the body to effectively pass certain electrolytes across the cells membranes.

While obviously it is recommended that people who exercise should replace 100 percent of the fluids lost, it is seldom done. The normal person will replace only about 50 percent during the exercise period. Dehydration of 4 percent of the body's weight will reduce one's endurance by 30 percent in temperate conditions but by as much as 50 percent when the weather is very warm.

Exercise in cold weather also requires adequate fluid intake. You must warm the air you breathe and maintain a normal body temperature. Moisture is lost to the drier cold air (you can see the moisture loss when your breath looks like steam in cold air). You will tend to produce more urine. These factors require you to take in more fluid. If you don't, your body will feel colder because your blood will not have sufficient volume to warm your skin effectively with the heat it picks up from the exercising muscles.

Dehydration due to excessive heat and/or inadequate fluid intake can cause serious heat-related illnesses. A sudden change in the heat or humidity where you practice or traveling to a warmer or more humid climate to compete can also cause problems. If you were to travel to India, Egypt, or the Caribbean to compete in a marathon, for example, it would probably take ten days to two weeks to acclimatize yourself to the warmer or more humid climate.

Among the changes that will probably occur in a high-heat environment are a reduced heart rate (due to less need for blood to heat the skin—resulting in less blood flow to the skin), an increase in the amount of blood plasma, increased sweating, perspiring earlier when exercising, increased salt losses, and the psychological adjustments made to the experience of greater heat and humidity.

Adequate fluid is essential to the functioning of an efficient body. When body fluids are reduced by sweating, less fluid is available in the blood and other tissues. This makes the body less efficient and, in some cases, can result in serious sickness or even death. To keep your body hydrated you should have frequent breaks for fluid intake. However, even frequent breaks seldom give an exerciser enough fluid. A person's thirst does not signal the true need for fluids.

The ingredients of sweat change as you exercise. At the beginning a number of salts are excreted. Sodium chloride (common table salt) as well as potassium, calcium, chromium, zinc, and magnesium salts can be lost. The initial sweat contains most of these salts but as the exercise continues, the amount of salts in the sweat may be reduced because some of the body's hormones come into play. Aldosterone, for example, conserves the body's sodium. Consequently the longer we exercise the more our sweat resembles pure water. And just as we vary in nearly every other area, we sweat differently as individuals. Some players sweat more or lose more salts than others.

A normal diet replaces all of the necessary elements lost in sweat. Drinking a single glass of orange or tomato juice replaces all or most of the calcium, potassium, and magnesium lost. Further, most of us have plenty of sodium in our daily diets.

Fluid replacement drinks on the market are not necessarily recommended. They vary considerably in their contents. Water, the most needed element, is slowed in its absorption if the drink contains other elements such as salts and some forms of sugar. Water alone is therefore often the recommended drink for fluid replacement—and it is certainly the least expensive. For those who want to replace water and sugars for energy the best drinks are those that contain glucose polymers (maltodextrins). Potassium and sodium may also need to be replaced. So if you are using fluid replacement drinks, check the label, then buy what you need—salts and/or sugars. Both caffeine (coffee, tea, and cola drinks) and alcohol dehydrate the body and should be avoided.

There is no question that adding carbohydrates, such as maltodextrins, to water is highly effective in replacing your body's fuel. In a study of marathon runners given either a high carbohydrate drink or a placebo every fifteen minutes during a run, those receiving the high carbohydrate drink were able to keep the blood sugar glycogen much higher during and after the run.

While water is generally recommended as the drink to replace lost perspiration, there are times when some electrolytes (sodium and potassium) must be replaced. Football players working in the heat of the summer sun in Texas or Arizona will probably need extra electrolytes. In such situations it may be wise to eat a diet higher than normal in potassium and, depending on the amount of sweat, some extra sodium. You might consume a drink with extra electrolytes, such as V-8 juice or orange juice, or a sport drink with these elements.

If you are exercising for more than fifteen minutes or exercising in the heat you must be conscious of your need for fluid. Even a minimal level of dehydration (less than 2 percent loss of body weight due to perspiration) impairs the cardiovascular and the heat regulating abilities of the body. Even when exercising for less than an hour, fluid replacement is essential.

Problems Caused by Heat

Heat cramps generally involve cramping of the legs, arms, or abdomen. The victim will be able to think clearly and will have a normal rectal temperature. The treatment is to give fluids with salt and possibly other minerals—as are found in most fluid replacement drinks. Heat cramps are particularly common among exercisers who are not yet in good physical condition and who are participating during warm days. There should be no problem in returning to activity the next day.

Heat exhaustion is generally caused by too little fluid or insufficient salts in the body. There are two types of heat exhaustion: water depletion heat exhaustion and salt depletion heat exhaustion.

Water depletion heat exhaustion is caused by insufficient water intake or excessive sweating. The symptoms may include intense thirst, weakness, chills, fast breathing, impaired judgment, nausea, a lack of muscular coordination, and/or dizziness. If untreated, heat exhaustion can develop into heat stroke—a rectal temperature of over 104°F (40°C). The immediate treatment is to give water or an electrolyte replacement drink. When the case is severe it may require intravenous fluid replacement. The skin will generally feel cool and somewhat moist.

Salt depletion heat exhaustion appears to be similar to heat cramps. This can occur when large volumes of sweat are replaced only with water. If a great deal of salt was lost in the perspiration it can affect muscle functioning. Salt depletion heat exhaustion is most likely to occur during the first five to ten days of exercising in the heat. The symptoms may include vomiting, nausea, inability to eat, diarrhea, a headache (particularly in the front of the head), weakness, a lower body temperature, and muscle cramps. Weight loss and thirst are not symptoms of this problem.

Heat stroke can be caused by heavy exercise just as it can by high air temperature. It is a very serious condition that can affect many of the organs. Heat stroke can occur when the interior organs of the body are heated above 106°F (42°C). At this temperature protein begins to break down. Enzymes are affected, as are the cell walls. When the cells cannot function effectively, the organ functioning is impaired.

In addition to a body temperature in excess of 104°F (40°C) there can be a rapid pulse (100 to 120 beats per minute) and low blood pressure. There may also be confusion, weakness, fatigue, delirium, or the victim may lapse into a coma. The confusion that may be exhibited is often confused with a head injury in contact sports. The skin color is grayish, indicating poor circulation, and the skin will be clammy. There may or may not be sweating. The pupils of the eyes may be very small.

Treatment for heat stroke requires the immediate cooling of the body. Don't wait for the hospital to treat the victim. It may be too late. Use ice packs to the neck and groin. Full immersion in a tub of cold water is better. An athlete who has experienced a heat stroke should not return to activity for at least a week or two.

To prevent these heat-related problems athletic trainers often require that athletes regain 80 percent of their fluid loss before leaving the locker room. So if an athlete weighed 150 pounds before the practice and 146 pounds afterward, for example, the trainer could require that the athlete take in enough fluids to bring the weight back to slightly over 149 pounds before leaving the facility.

18

Performance Enhancing and Reducing Substances

There are a number of substances that can increase one's performance. Some have no negative effects on the body, such as vitamins and minerals, and some have severe negative effects like steroids and amphetamines. Substances that help one to work better or more efficiently are called ergogenic, which means "work enhancing" or "energy producing." So ergogenic aids are whatever facilitates progress toward strength or bulk development and aerobic or anaerobic work. They can range from legal vitamin pills to illegal steroids.

In a study on Olympic athletes, the athletes were asked if they would take a drug that would guarantee them an Olympic medal but would kill them in five years. Over 50 percent of them said they would take that drug. That is scary, especially when you are coaching a game such as football.

Football is a game of strength and speed. That does not mean that the strongest and fastest will always win, however. We have detailed at length how technique can overcome a stronger and faster player. But you still want to be at your legal peak—neither chemically up nor down. We detailed the possibility for vitamin or mineral supplementation and the effects of a high-fat diet and the ingestion of caffeinated drinks. Your performance will certainly be enhanced by a high carbohydrate diet with sufficient protein. But let us look at some other substances.

Creatine

Creatine phosphate is a necessary part of the animal energy system. (See Chapter 15 for a brief explanation of the anaerobic energy system.) Creatine is synthesized from the amino acids methionine, tryptophan, valine and other essential amino acids. It is the only ergogenic (energy producing) substance that is today recognized as safe and effective.

Creatine is found in two forms in the body. Approximately 25 to 40 percent is in the free creatine form (Crfree), while the remaining 60 to 75 percent is in the phosphorylated form, creatine phosphate (CP). It is the creatine phosphate that releases its phosphate molecule to resynthsize the ATP so that the energy source is available to contract the muscles during exercise.

The free creatine may also become creatine phosphate if it picks up a phosphate. The daily turnover rate of creatine is approximately 2 grams per day, which is replenished by both food and supplementation and by the body's synthesis of creatine. While more creatine is found in the stronger fast twitch muscles, the slow twitch fibers are able to resynthesize the ATP through the use of oxygen (aerobic). Most research has found the only side effect associated with creatine phosphate supplementation appears to be a small increase in body mass, which is most likely due to water retention.

Since there is generally not enough creatine phosphate in the muscles, some strength athletes have been taking creatine monohydrate as a supplement. It has been found that creatine supplements improve anaerobic recovery, energy, and power by 10 to 19.6 percent. Water in the muscle cells is essential to the use of ATP and creatine. Without sufficient water intake the energy production is hindered and cramping can occur. Creatine monohydrate is not easily absorbed by the body—only about 10 percent is absorbed, so it has a great deal of waste. The amount not absorbed moves through the intestine and on to be excreted in the feces or through the kidneys. This could theoretically cause kidney problems.

High-level scientific studies (several hundred in the last seventeen years) have used twenty grams of creatine monohydrate per person per day for five days (the loading period) then two to three grams per day. This will give you all you need, if you were not eating enough protein to make sufficient creatine. More than the two to three grams a day does not help. Recommendations for athletes vary from two to five grams per day (without a loading period). More than that level would be excreted and could theoretically cause kidney problems—though none have yet been reported. More creatine than the two to five grams per day (depending on how much meat protein is consumed in the diet) would not help the athlete. It helps only athletes who create their energy anaerobically (without oxygen). It would not help long distance runners who use oxygen for their energy (aerobic).

We are not recommending supplementation for the average person, but for the elite level athlete it seems to show promise. If you were to supplement creatine it must be done correctly. The only side effects reported have been muscle cramping, probably from the increased fluid in the muscle, and some diarrhea and gas. If any danger exists it would probably be by taking more than the recommended dose. There is no evidence that taking more than the recommended amount would help.

To summarize current thinking on the matter of creatine supplementation we will cite the findings of the American College of Sports Medicine Roundtable:

- It can increase muscle phosphocreatine (PCr) content, but not in all individuals
- A high dose of twenty grams, which is common in research studies, is not necessary because a longer term use of three grams a day will eventually give the same increase
- Ingesting fairly large amounts of carbohydrates at the same time as ingesting the creatine will increase the uptake by the muscles
- Exercise performance involving short periods of extremely powerful activity (sprinting, jumping, etc.) can be enhanced, especially during repeated bouts of activity
- Creatine supplementation does not increase maximal isometric strength, the rate of maximal force production, or aerobic exercise performance
- Most of the evidence has been obtained from healthy young adult male subjects with mixed athletic ability and training status; less research information is available related to the alterations due to age and gender
- Creatine supplementation leads to weight gain within the first few days, likely due to water retention related to creatine uptake in the muscle

- Creatine supplementation is associated with an enhancement of strength in strength-training programs, a response not independent from the initial weight gain, but may be related to a greater volume and intensity of training that can be achieved
- There is no definitive evidence that creatine supplementation causes gastrointestinal, renal, and/or muscle cramping complications
- The potential acute effects of high-dose creatine supplementation on body fluid balance has not been fully investigated
- Ingestion of creatine before or during exercise is not recommended

On the negative side, extensive use of creatine monohydrate has generated sufficient danger signals to have creatine supplementation banned in France, pending more definitive studies of its safety and efficacy. The reasoning behind the decision by the French Food Safety Agency is the conservative view that healthy people should not take anything that may be a risk to their health that does not have solidly proven benefit. Among the safety concerns of the French are a number of reactions which people have reported, none of which are known yet to be caused specifically by a creatine supplement (a brief list includes headache, anxiety, high blood pressure, fatigue, cramping, and death). Whether these are the result of taking creatine monohydrate or taking too much of the supplement is not known. Safety will be more likely to be evaluated when a water soluble type of creatine is generally available.

Steroids

The use of steroids used to be a problem in the NFL. There were documented cases of players using them and then having major health problems. Lyle Alzado died of brain cancer after admitting that he had used many different types of steroids over the years.

Steve Corson, formerly of the Pittsburgh Steelers, died of heart complications that were believed to be caused by steroids. There are many others who have had numerous other health problems caused from steroids. A number of bodybuilders who have used steroids have abused their kidneys so much that for the rest of their lives they will have to report to a hospital three days a week for several hours of treatment. The kidneys were overworked in having to process so many toxic substances.

Among their many harmful side effects are leukemia (blood cancer), liver cancer, and other liver problems, in addition to the following:

- Premature closing of the growth plates in the bones, stopping growth in height
- Bone brittleness, often resulting in breaks
- Decreasing testicle size in men (and reduced reproductive capacity)
- Breast soreness and enlargement (males)
- High blood pressure
- Lower amounts of high density lipoprotein (HDL) in the blood, which increases the possibility of hardening the arteries
- Increased blood clotting
- Abnormal enlargement of the heart
- Risk of sudden cardiac arrest
- Kidney damage
- Liver inflammation, which can result in cancer
- Impaired thyroid and pituitary functions
- Increase in nervous tension
- Problems with the prostate gland
- Impotence (males)
- Oily skin
- Skin rashes and acne
- Increased body hair
- Thinning hair on scalp
- Gastrointestinal problems
- Muscle cramps or muscle spasms
- Headaches
- Dizziness or drowsiness
- Nosebleeds

There are other non-life-threatening problems caused by steroids. Pulled muscles and broken bones are much more common among people who take them. Players have literally ripped muscle from the bone because the muscles were stronger than the ligaments that were supposed to hold them to the bone. Injuries take a longer time to heal when using steroids. Even the common cold will take longer to leave people who are taking steroids.

In the late 1990s the National Football League banned steroids and now tests for them. This is not a random test done only at training camp or some other designated time. They are tested throughout the entire season. If a positive test is found, that player is suspended without pay for four games. The NFL realized what a huge potential problem steroids are, so football was the first team sport to be so proactive in ridding itself of the problem.

The Giants drafted Eric Dorsey, a defensive lineman out of Notre Dame, in the first round in 1986. Eric was 6′6″and 290 pounds with 7 percent body fat. His arms were about twenty-one inches around. He was huge. He was fast. (He

When I was playing for the Giants, our team did not have a problem with steroids. In 1986, our Super Bowl year, we had only one person who was taking steroids at the start of the year, and he stopped using them during the season. The Giants were a great team that used speed, quickness, and strength, but we did not have to use steroids to get these attributes. Good old hard work was what got it done.

We have heard of players or other "people in the know" who said that 60 percent of all players in the league were using steroids before testing came in. That is just wrong. They either said it to justify their taking them, or they lost their spot to someone and wanted to blame it on the other person being on steroids. There were teams that had what could be considered widespread use of steroids, with probably 30 percent of the linemen using them. The amazing thing was that the teams that had the problem were generally teams with bad records. During training camp we practiced against one team for three days prior to our preseason game against them. It was obvious who was using when you looked at them. They showed signs of being puffy, retaining water, and had bad acne, especially on their backs. They were open about it since it was not a banned substance at the time. We played another "cellar dweller" during the year in which many of their players had friends on the Giants. A player from that team told my teammate about six of their linemen were using the stuff.

The bad teams were looking for a quick fix, the easy way to get to the top. They thought that since steroids can make you bigger and stronger, then if a bunch of them used, they would have a better team. It didn't work. A team is only as good as the people on it. If you have a group of people working for a common goal who believe in each other, that is much more powerful than a few guys who are strong. The easy way rarely works in the long run, and it proved out for these teams.

There was an offensive lineman who came out of Michigan State in the 1990s. *Sports Illustrated* did a cover story on him. He was huge. He physically beat up everyone in college, regularly pancaking his opponents. Players were afraid to go against him. *Sports Illustrated* detailed how much he ate every day (a massive amount) and how hard he worked out. He lifted incredible amounts. Everyone suspected how he was able to work out as hard as he did—steroids—but without proof (colleges did not test for them) nothing was said publicly. He was the second player drafted by the Green Bay Packers. He came into the NFL just as it started its steroid testing. He had to go off the stuff. He started losing weight in dramatic amounts. A former teammate of mine was with the Packers when he got there. He said that this player even went so far as to put weights in his pockets during weigh-ins so it didn't look like he was losing as much weight. After going off steroids, he was never the player he was when he was on them. He lost about 20 percent of his strength, common for steroid users who go off. He was still stronger than about 90 percent of the players he played against, but because he didn't see himself as strong any longer, he played like he was weak. He was not a good player for them, rarely playing except after the game's conclusion was already determined. He ended up having some very serious health problems and was forced to leave the league.

I was a pretty good player for the Giants. If I had not gotten sick in 1987, I would have had a very good chance to go to the Pro Bowl. I was 6'6" and weighed 285 pounds, the tallest and heaviest player on the team. The most I ever bench-pressed was 360 pounds, but I could power clean 365. You do not have to be an animal to play the game. Every year we would have guys come into camp that were huge, with muscles bulging upon muscles. I would look at these guys and wonder how I was going to compete. But when it came time to hit someone, they couldn't get it done. We had a saying for people like this—"Look like Tarzan, play like Jane."

was a natural physical specimen—no steroids.) I had to block him. If he took an inside move on a pass rush, it was like riding a rodeo bull. But if you could get him going upfield, you could literally block him with one finger. He was so big that he had no body control and could not change directions once he got going in a certain direction. This just goes to show that you do not have to be incredibly strong in order to play the game.

We have heard about a very disturbing trend happening in the high schools. More and more high school players are using steroids to get stronger. Some are even encouraged by their coaches to do it. If you have a kid who is increasing his lifts every single week or is putting on weight at an unnatural rate, take him aside and question him on how he is doing it. I strongly believe that coaches should have a no-steroid policy and cut any player found to be using. Users will be a detriment to the team and to themselves. They will use peer pressure to get others on the team to use. You may think that you will have a better team if you have players using steroids, but as I have shown, this is not the case

If you go to any gym, there will probably be someone there who can get steroids or knows how to get them. Everything possible should be done to stop this trend. Call the police if you know of this going on.

Vince Lombardi said, "Winning isn't everything, but preparing to win is." But I am sure he would not condone the use of steroids in order to help his team prepare to win. He was a guy who believed in hard work and determination, not in finding a quick fix that was illegal. The easy way is very rarely the right way.

Uncommon Facts About Common Psychoactive Drugs

We all know the basics about alcohol and tobacco so that we can counsel our players. But there are some facts that are not so commonly known.

Psychoactive drugs work by interfering with the neurotransmitters (the chemicals that transmit the nerve impulse from one nerve to another primarily in the brain). Some neurotransmitters work in the stimulating nerves, others in the relaxing nerves. The many types of psychoactive drugs work differently, some increasing the amount of neurotransmitter, some decreasing it and some mimicking it. With over two hundred neurotransmitters it is easy to see how the various drugs can affect us, making us more excited, more calm, or putting us to sleep. By changing the natural level of normal brain chemicals, psychoactive drugs can negatively affect many nerve abilities such as remembering and sleeping, and can increase mental illness, anxiety, nervousness and concentration.

Caffeine

Caffeine is a mild stimulant ("upper") drug that can lead to both physical and psychological dependence to a very limited degree. However on the positive side it seems to help learning and it helps the body to mobilize fats faster so it can aid in energy production. It was on the International Olympic Committee's banned substances list but is no longer.

Tobacco

Tobacco is the second most addictive drug after cocaine. It is the only drug that has both an upper and a downer effect, so when a person withdraws from it he gets the upper effect of a downer withdrawal (such as alcohol or heroin, but not as strong) and the downer effect of withdrawing from an upper drug (such as cocaine). Nicotine releases adrenaline that gives smokers the upper effect, and the nicotine acts like a calming brain neurotransmitter in the synapses of the nerves. This is what gives the downer or calming effect. So while neither its upper nor downer effects are extremely sharp, the combination makes withdrawal very difficult. Of course it's well known that nicotine raises blood pressure, which is negative for athletes, and that the tars reduce one's ability to absorb oxygen from the air into the alveoli of the lungs. This of course hurts the aerobic aspect of energy production. The calming effect of the nicotine reduces the anaerobic ability by increasing the calming effect on the nerves.

Alcohol

Alcohol is highly addictive for some people. It also adds unwanted empty calories and can deaden the nerve fibers, which make it more difficult to effectively coordinate movement. Because it is a depressant, in terms of its effect on the nervous system, it reduces the effect of the energy producing system.

Marijuana

Marijuana has the same tar effect as tobacco, with one smoked joint having the same amount of tars as a pack of smoked cigarettes. Since the THC in marijuana has a half-life of seven to ten days, compared to a half-life of several hours for alcohol, the effects of a smoked joint last for days; because the THC, as LSD and PCP, is fat soluble it stays in the tissues for weeks, so repeated use of the drug increases the amount held in the body. Most drugs are water soluble, so they leave the body more quickly. Like tobacco it reduces the aerobic potential of the cardiopulmonary system. Like alcohol it acts as a calming medium, so it slows down the anaerobic potential.

Stimulants

Stimulants such as cocaine, methamphetamine (speed) and its relative ecstasy (MDMA, or 3-4 methylenedioxymethamphetamine), and ephedra have occasionally been used by athletes to gain extra energy. They are harmful for athletes, as for others. Users show poor memory and a higher than normal body temperature, which is particularly dangerous in warmer climates and can lead to death. They may also experience increased nausea, depression, blurred vision, muscle tension, nerve damage, and a number of other effects that are negative for athletes.

Several years ago one professional team had a number of players using amphetamines. The stimulating effects had them hitting harder but their brains were so disturbed that they kept hitting the wrong people. Uppers are obviously not for football players.

Depressants

Depressants such as heroin, morphine, and various sleep producing drugs are used in the medical profession to ease physical pain, as may be necessary after a surgery. But many people take these drugs to eliminate mental pain because they can't face life. Any of these drugs would have obvious negative effects for athletes and would end their careers because their sedative effects would take away all athletic skills and strength.

Any psychoactive drug, whether it is alcohol, LSD, or any other drug, will have negative effects on any athlete by changing the body's natural balance.

19

The Mental Side of Offensive Line Play

Yogi Berra said that baseball is 90 percent mental and the other half is physical. While this is a true "Yogiism," it has a lot of truth. There is no dispute that football is a physical game, much more so than baseball, but the mental side of it is still extremely important. At the end of a season, while I was physically exhausted, I would actually be more mentally exhausted. Many games are won because of mental preparation. A player who is mentally prepared will not make the key mistake in a game. We will discuss more about mental preparation later in the chapter. First let's discuss the mental makeup of a successful offensive lineman.

The Mental Makeup of a Successful Lineman

When dividing the players on your team by position, you take into account certain physical attributes necessary for each position. Your fastest people will be receivers or running backs. Your most aggressive players will be linebackers. The more passive players, especially if they have some size, are delegated to the offensive line.

Some people think that pass blocking is a passive activity. While it is a reactive activity, you still need to be aggressive with it. You do have to take the blows of the rusher, such as slaps and bull rushing, but you can also punch out when the time is right. Run blocking is very aggressive.

The biggest problem in getting people to play the offensive line is that it is by far the least glamorous position on the field. The quarterback is generally the star player who gets all the glory. The running backs carry the ball. The receivers get to run free and catch the ball. Defensive players make tackles and interceptions. Offensive linemen get to block. They get to open holes so the running backs can run to glory. They get to pass block so the star quarterback has time to throw the ball to the open receivers. Offensive linemen are the grunts of the football world. If you have a kid who constantly needs attention and glory, do not let him play the offensive line.

Even if you are a great offensive lineman, no statistics are kept to prove how good you are—except for the coaches' grades. The press has absolutely no idea about line play and who is playing well or playing sensationally. They only know by being told by coaches or scouts who is doing well or who is not playing up to par.

There is much more to being a successful offensive lineman than not wanting the limelight. They are generally the smarter people on the team. Every year at the NFL scouting combines, the offensive linemen score the highest on the

There generally were two instances when I would be interviewed by the press: when I played against Reggie White because he was the Eagles' star player, or when something went wrong. On Wednesday, our first day of the workweek and the first day we had to talk to the press, if I was playing Reggie, I would have about five or six reporters around my locker at lunch. They would ask all the usual questions each time I played him. It was boring, but at least I got some attention.

If I had a holding call I would get interviewed about what I did. Or if there were many sacks on the quarterback or we couldn't get the running game going the press would come and talk. The only time you get your name or number said during a game is if there is a penalty against you. The less you hear about an offensive lineman, the better he is playing.

Wonderlick Test, which is the test the NFL uses to measure intelligence. Yes, they score higher than the quarterbacks.

In college, the center and I were both engineering majors, as were two of the backups. With the Giants, Parcells called us the "Suburbanites" because we all had regular off-season jobs that you find in suburbia. I graduated in industrial engineering and was working in the field during the off-season. Chris Godfrey, who played guard next to me, had a business degree, but when he retired he went back and got his law degree. Bart Oates, the center, was going to law school during the off-season. Billy Ard was a stockbroker, and Brad Benson owned a Jaguar car dealership.

When you go through a locker room, you can generally tell the offensive linemen's lockers. They will be neater and more organized than the others. My wife may not agree that I am a neat person, but linemen tend to be more organized. They also tend to be punctual. O-linemen are always on time for meetings and practice. I do not remember an offensive lineman ever being fined while I was with the Giants. They are more regimented than other people. My wife says they are "anal." They tend to be detailed oriented. They are usually the most coachable group of players, taking suggestions and trying them without question. They tend to be more open-minded. They are generally more conservative, not partying as much as other positions. Certainly there are exceptions, but linemen do tend to show those qualities more than other players.

On the field, they must play with a controlled aggression. Always being in control is very important for offensive linemen. In Chapter 9, it was emphasized that one must be in control when there is chaos going on all around. This not easy, but it is a sign of a good offensive lineman. You have to have tunnel vision, blocking out all that is around and focusing on your assignment. Keeping the body in control and balanced at all times is essential.

I would play at Giants Stadium with seventy-eight thousand screaming maniac Giants fans, and I wouldn't hear a thing except for the quarterback and my teammates' calls.

There does have to be a certain killer instinct as well. You want to dominate your opponent. This comes from physically and mentally beating him. The offensive lineman has to want to hit and be hit. We talked elsewhere in the book about the bodybuilder types who try to play football. Many linemen either don't want to hit anyone or are afraid of getting hurt. A player who is out trying to not get hurt is the person who is most likely to get hurt. By avoiding contact the player will be more likely to take an unexpected hit that results in injury.

A little bit of a mean streak is also a good thing, as long as it can be controlled. It can add to the intensity of the player. It only becomes a detriment if it causes the player to do something stupid and take a penalty or not do his assignment because he was out to get on someone he was not supposed to.

I am by nature a very laid-back person. It took me a while to develop that killer instinct. It is something that can be learned. As a young player I was not aggressive, but as I got bigger and stronger and started having some success, it became enjoyable to flatten someone or get in a bit of a skirmish. It is a good thing for players to be two different people on and off the field. A person who is always aggressive and high-strung both on and off the field will burn out and also be a person who is more likely to have problems off the field. There were some players on the Giants who were like this, and they tended to get into trouble. I was two different people on and off the field. On the field I was very intense and competitive. But I had to work to get myself this way. Off the field I was very noncompetitive, and I still am. I do not like playing golf for money, and I enjoy a friendly card game more than a competitive one.

While being controlled and aggressive, it is also important for an offensive lineman to not show emotion if he is beaten. The natural tendency when you get beaten is to yell, curse, or show body language that you are upset. Defensive players will feed off of this and just keep coming harder and tougher. Parcells preached this all the time with us, sometimes being more upset with us showing emotion than with getting beaten. I really learned this when Jack Youngblood beat me so badly back in 1984. He mentally beat me, and then he

A player's emotions affect how he plays. I played against a player for the St. Louis Cardinals and Cleveland Browns by the name of Al "Bubba" Baker. If Al's mouth wasn't moving, then his heart wasn't beating. Most big guys don't talk, but he sure did. I was playing against him and early in the game he was going nuts on me, pushing after the play and taking swipes at me. This was very unlike him. Finally I said, "Are we going to do this crap all day, or are we going to play football?" He said that I had poked him in the eye on the first play and he was mad at me for doing it. I said that I certainly didn't mean to, I had never done it before. If he still wants to play crazy, I will play crazy also. But why don't we just play football. He said, "Fine. Let's play football." I didn't have a problem with him the rest of the game.

physically beat me. I showed how upset I was at being beaten and he just fed on that negative energy and kept getting stronger.

Handling Trash Talk

Linemen on both sides of the ball often encounter trash talking. Your opponent may be talking about what he is going to do to you or to your mother. Obviously he is more interested in his own ego than in playing the game. What he doesn't know is that when he is talking about one thing he cannot be thinking of his assignment. If he can get you to think about what he is saying you have been brought down to his level and you will both be less effective football players.

When you encounter a trash talker it is essential that you concentrate on your assignment. Think only about who and how you will block. If you concentrate hard on your job you won't hear the idiot on the other side of the line of scrimmage. This will make you more effective and give you the upper hand in your encounter with him. You noticed we did not say to "not think about what he is saying." This would actually make you hear him. The key is to think only about your job and exactly how you will do it. So always think of your job only—trash talk or not.

Visualization

Mental preparation for a game is very important. You must get yourself mentally ready to go out and make your body do things that it really doesn't want to do. By nature, humans want to avoid pain. The body will naturally react to avoid hits. You can overcome these tendencies with proper mental preparation. If you visualize the game in your head, making all the plays, the hits, and taking the hits, it will be easier to do these when the time comes in the game. Since your mind is used to performing these things and not feeling the consequences because of the visualization, it will more easily allow your body to do the necessary things on the field. For a game on Sunday, I started visualizing the game on the previous Wednesday.

Every elite athlete uses visualization to get ready for a competition. In visualization the user can see the activity from the outside (external imagery) or feel himself performing it from the inside (internal imagery). In external visualization you see yourself doing whatever you are going to do. The famous golfer Jack Nicklaus called it "going to the movies" when he visualized himself performing his golf swing. You can visualize yourself by watching yourself pull and trap, perform a drive block, counter a pass rusher trying to "swim" you, or make a downfield block. You can also use internal visualization by *feeling* yourself doing the activity. Psychologists have found that when we feel ourselves doing an activity we actually have contractions in the muscles we use when doing that activity. So whether it is skiing, serving a tennis ball, or making a pull and zeroing in on a defensive lineman's numbers as we mentally make contact with him—visualization makes you a better lineman.

Imagery, or visualization, is mental practice. Much of the early work in developing the technique was done in the United States, but it was the Eastern bloc countries that refined and applied this knowledge. The basic principles, however, have been instinctively employed to some degree by many athletes for years.

Greg Louganis, the Olympic champion diver, started his mental practice of a dive with the same kind of external visualization, then he felt himself doing the dive—internal visualization. He also found it helpful to play appropriate music while he mentally performed the dive.

You can apply these techniques to your individual skills. If you know that when you run block your toes are turned outward, you can mentally practice thinking of them as turned inward. If you know that in your pass protection your head is too far forward, you can mentally set it back and feel yourself in the proper blocking position. If you have trouble blocking a certain type of pass rush, such as a club and swim, you can mentally practice the correct moves to counteract it.

Coaches should encourage their athletes to mentally practice their individual skills and their team responsibilities. When an upcoming opponent has been scouted and individual or team tendencies are learned, the coach should work the individual or the team through the desired skill or reaction pattern. The coach can have the players in a quiet room, eyes closed, then mentally take them through the skills, reactions, or team play desired. Players get far more repetitions in doing an action mentally than they do on the field. Once the players have learned this skill the coach can tell them what skills or reactions are most important to mentally practice. The athletes can then do this mental practicing at home.

> We would watch film of the team we were going to play against on Wednesday and go over the personnel so I knew who I was going to be blocking and how he played. Before I went to sleep I would lie in bed with my eyes closed and "see" that player make a play, beating me on a pass rush. Then I would replay that same move and visualize myself countering the move. I would do this for every pass rush move that he had. I would do this over and over. As the game got closer, I would spend more and more time visualizing. By the time Saturday night came around, my wife Heidi said that I was "in the zone," where I spent most of my time playing the game in my head. If we went out to eat on a Saturday night, she would pick a restaurant that did not have those little candles on the tables because if they were there I would just stare into them and go into almost a trance. She would ask me questions and talk to me, but I would not hear her.

The Giants generally went into a game with about fifteen running plays. The defense might have up to ten different fronts that we had to be prepared to block each of those fifteen running plays against. That is 150 potential combinations. We did not have enough time to go over each of those situations during the week of practice. We would run our most likely plays against the defense we thought we were most likely to see for that formation and situation. Of the 150 potential combos, we probably saw only about 40 of them live in practice. And that was only one time against players that played differently than the ones we would see on Sunday. We had to be mentally ready for any of those combinations during the game. You cannot call time-out because the line doesn't know how to block a certain front. That meant that we had to spend a lot of time away from the field getting mentally prepared for anything that our opponent could throw at us.

When you see a team making many mental mistakes and getting stupid penalties, I think this is because they are not mentally prepared to play. If they had been doing their studying and visualization these things would not be happening. Coach Fassel, who was the Giants' coach until 2004, told me about a player who messed up a play they practiced every single week against the same defense. It was a goal line play where the front-side guard pulls and is supposed to turn up into the hole and block the inside linebacker. The fullback blocks the force man on the line of scrimmage. In this case the guard pulled and blocked the force man, leaving the inside backer free to make the play. Fassel couldn't understand how this player made the mistake. I think it was because he was not spending enough time away from the field thinking about the game and his assignments.

The problem is there are so many distractions out there such as computers, video games, girlfriends, and many others. You must impress upon the players that if football is important, then they will have to work at it both on and off the field. It is essential that to be the best player you can be you have to think about football and give up some of the other distractions. School should not be considered a distraction, but a necessity that also will take time.

The Mental Side of Coaching Linemen

How should you coach offensive linemen? There are many theories on this. Bill Parcells's greatest quality was that whatever you had in you, he could get out of you. Some guys he would take off to the side, put his arm around them, and tell them nicely what he wanted them to do. Other guys he would kick in the butt to get his point across. I always thought I should have been one of the guys he put his arm around, but I was always one of the guys he kicked in the butt.

Parcells is famous for playing head games with his players. This goes for everyone from the star quarterback to the last man on the roster. To this day my wife still does not like him because of the way I would come home some days with my tail between my legs. Sometimes I felt like I couldn't even put one foot in front of the other without tripping, he had me so messed up.

Unfortunately, I do think that offensive linemen are generally the guys that you can kick in the butt. Because they are smarter and need to be tougher than some of the other positions, they can take the criticism. I think linemen are more coachable and will take direction better. Be tough with them, expect a lot out of them, but don't berate them.

If a person makes a mistake and doesn't learn from it, then he has made two mistakes. Repeated mental mistakes show a lack of discipline and attention. Someone who makes many mental mistakes should consider a position other than offensive line. Let him play defense. Nothing will bring an offense to a screaming halt faster than missed assignments by the line.

Every error made is a learning opportunity. You, as a coach, should see it as such. Make sure every mistake is pointed out and corrected. Most people, including the coach, tend to follow the football on a play and don't see the little things in the line away from the ball that can truly make the difference in the play. One coach should be assigned to watch the linemen away from the ball to make sure they are doing the right thing. Leave plenty of time in practice for making corrections, especially for young players. If the player learns it wrong and is not corrected, then he will continue to make the same mistake over and over until it is a bad habit.

What We Can Learn from Sport Psychology

Sport psychology grew out of general psychology, particularly out of educational psychology, which studies how we can learn more effectively. The first major study looking at mental skills in elite athletes was done as late as 1987. In this chapter we are looking how you can improve your line play. This is important for both the coaches and the athletes.

In a study of middle school athletes done at Northern Illinois University it was found that the goals of the athletes changed over the season. The way the athletes perceived how well they had mastered their sports skills changed as they moved through the competitive season. The conclusion was that sport offers a different environment than is found in academic or "outside world" settings, so general psychology and educational psychology principles may have to be adapted for the sport setting.

Emotions also needed to be addressed by sport psychology. But some sport psychologists have recognized that top-level athletes not only need to be able to control their emotions and concentrate on their techniques, they must also be geared to perfection. High-level success is the aim of effective sport psychology. We are not looking at the "average" person as we do in general psychology.

A study of the very top male and female elite athletes found that when comparing Olympic and world championship medal winners with elite college and top junior athletes the highest-level athletes:

- Were more able to handle precompetition anxiety
- Were more mentally balanced
- Were able to concentrate better both before and during competition
- Were more self-confident
- Were better able to imagine themselves doing their event
- Were less affected by external (such as a coach's) motivational techniques
- Found more meaning in their sport

Whether you are competing with yourself in the weight room or competing against others on the practice or game field, your mental preparation is essential. Long before sport psychologists entered the scene, athletes were using the psychological technique of imagery, mentally practicing before the competition. Goal setting, another essential of the sport psychologists, has been implicit in every athlete's desire for higher-level performances. What sport psychologists have done, however, is to make us aware of how to do it better.

Mental Conditioning

There is an important side of our conditioning that is mental rather than physical. The mental aspects of conditioning include:

- Setting goals and developing the proper intensity of motivation
- Taking advantage of the mental benefits that result from the release of endorphins (which produce a feeling of pleasure)
- Using mental imagery to increase the ability to perform
- Learning to concentrate during the workout and during competition
- Learning to relax between the segments of our practices, between practice sessions, and even to relax during competition
- Understanding the mental factors that are associated with athletic success, many of which are specific to each individual athlete
- Understanding and controlling our anxieties, both inside and outside of sport
- Understanding our most efficient level of arousal for a sport performance

Set Goals for Your Sport—and Your Life

In any worthwhile area of our lives we should have well-defined goals. The attainment of those goals should be measurable. If I say, "My goal is to run the hundred meters in 12.2 seconds," it is a measurable goal. But if I say, "My goal is to be happy," it is not effectively measured. If I break down what I mean by happiness I should be able to make it more measurable. If I say, "To be happy I want three close friends, ten close acquaintances, a B average in school, and a varsity letter on the football team." All of these goals are measurable.

As an example of goal setting, here are some goals you might consider for your strength development program. Each must be measurable. Typical goals for a weight-training program are:

- To develop general strength fitness for everyday living
- To develop strength in an injured joint
- To increase lean body mass and reduce body fat
- To develop better posture
- To develop strength and techniques specifically for competitions
- To develop muscular endurance
- To develop more speed and power
- To develop strength specifically for improved blocking ability

Whatever your goal, it should be specific and attainable. So choose a goal that can be measured: "I want to be able to improve my bench press by ten pounds." "I want to decrease my forty-yard sprint time by two-tenths of a second."

Some goals are individual, some should be team oriented. The individual goals could be "I will be able to hold off the pass rusher for 3.5 seconds." "I will bring my resting pulse to fifty-five beats per minute by June 1." "I will be able to run forty yards in under 5.5 seconds by May 1." Individual goals relating to the team might be "I will speak to one new person each day at practice until I know everyone on the squad." "I will invite ten members of the team to my house for a barbecue." "I will raise fifty dollars in the team car wash." Team goals should be set by the team. They might include "We will allow no quarterback sacks in this week's game." "Every rushing play will gain at least four yards." "We will have no blocked punts."

There is an old Irish proverb that says, "If you don't know where you're going you won't know if you get there." Goal setting is an absolute primary starting point for every athlete.

Rehearse Success

In any mental rehearsal, whether for a life goal, a conditioning goal, or a sport-specific goal, it is essential to think positively. Concentrating on failure will produce it. If you concentrate on success, you are, in effect, practicing to succeed. Successful golfers have long practiced this idea of positive visualization. They don't look at the water hazard or the sand trap, they visualize where they want to hit the ball—and think positively.

Concentrate

When you concentrate, you narrow the focus of your thought power to one object or task, or even just one element of an object or task. Thus, a golfer may concentrate on just one small part of the golf ball before swinging to hit it. A weight trainer may concentrate on the pressure against the hands or on one muscle group before and during the exercise. A run blocker may concentrate on the lower edge of the near number of the defender.

Build Motivation

The intensity and extent of one's desire to accomplish any of these goals is called *motivation*. The degree of motivation can be measured by how fervently the goal or goals are pursued. It has been said that "a person isn't what he says but rather what he does." As a person successfully accomplishes goals in life, as in athletics, that person's self-confidence increases. And in sport, self-confidence is a major factor for success. This is a reason that coaches should not "put down" their athletes. While the coach may think that sarcasm stirs the athlete to achieve more, in reality it generally is counterproductive because it decreases the athlete's self-confidence. Encouragement is a far more effective psychological tool for helping people to succeed.

The Mental Benefits of Strength Training

Since we have spent some time on effective strength training in Chapter 15, it seems appropriate that we mention the mental benefits of such training here. Both off-field conditioning and on-field practice and competition have positive mental benefits. A higher level of physical fitness helps people feel better and cope better with mental stresses. Their self-concept is enhanced not only by the development of a better physique but also by the feeling of success that comes from accomplishing fitness goals.

Mental Training Works

Dr. Charles Garfield relates his experience as the subject of an experiment in the mental approach to weight lifting. As a weight lifter who met several Soviet psychologists at an international meeting, he doubted the validity of the results the Soviets had reported for mental training for weight lifting.

The Soviets asked him about his maximum bench press. He said it was 365 pounds, eight years earlier when he was in serious training. They asked his most recent bench press max, and he said 280. Then they asked how long he thought it would take to train to again reach his maximum. He said, "At least nine months." With this information the Soviets were ready to prove their position.

They asked him to attempt a 300-pound press. To his great surprise, he succeeded—barely. Then they directed his relaxation using advanced techniques and had him deeply relaxed for forty minutes. They added 65 pounds to the bar and had him visualize lifting it. They had him mentally rehearse every aspect of the lift, from the feeling in the muscles to the sounds that he made while lifting. The process was repeated until he felt totally confident in what was about to happen. He concentrated on the lift and made it—equaling his lifetime best.

The Winner's Edge

You can gain so much more than your competition if you mentally practice your skills correctly. Mentally practice every move you may make. Watch the films of your opponent to be able to anticipate the types of pass rushes and run escapes he makes so that you can better control your battle.

20

Overcoming Adversity

On every single play during a football game, there is someone on the other side of the ball trying to stop you from doing your job. On every play you have to overcome some type of adversity. As a cancer survivor, I know a little about overcoming adversity.

The Giants had just won Super Bowl XXI in January of 1987. I was the starting right tackle on this team. I was on top of the world. But not for long. I worked out hard that off-season, as did the rest of the team. We wanted to repeat that following season.

During that training camp I was having some serious problems with my left shoulder. It was very weak. The more I used it the weaker it got. It got so bad that when I tried to hold out my arm straight in front of me for a trainer to test the strength, he could push my arm down by pushing on it with just his little finger. I took some time off to let it rest, but when I came back it just got weak again. Parcells wanted me to tough it out. I played the first preseason game in New England with one arm (and my all-important inside arm at that). I told Parcells I was going to get someone killed because I couldn't use it. The doctors decided to do a scope of the shoulder to get rid of some of the bone spurs and other things that were inflaming the shoulder. I went to the Hospital for Special Surgery to have this done.

They wanted to do a presurgery chest x-ray for their records. I told them that I had just had one in late May at mini camp. They insisted that I have it, and it was a good thing they did. That night, the team doctor, Russ Warren, came to my room and said they found a mass in my chest and the shoulder surgery would have to be put off for a while. They wanted to do a surgery to see what it was in my chest. The next day they wheeled me through a tunnel under 70th Street in Manhattan to NYU Medical Center where they were going to do the surgery to see what I had. I didn't ask any questions about the surgery, figuring they would do a small incision in my chest to get at the mass. I was wrong. They did what is called a *thoracotomy*, where they made an incision about twelve inches long, starting on my right side about halfway down my ribcage and then back around to the back, ending up by my shoulder blade. They took out a five-inch piece of rib and collapsed my lung to get at the mass. I woke up with a tube in my chest and the incision stapled shut with metal staples. I learned to start asking questions at this point.

A few days later, they informed my wife and me that I had Hodgkin's disease, a cancer of the lymph node system. If I had to have a cancer, they said this was the good one to have since it is the most treatable. I was in the hospital for a week after the surgery. After I got out my new doctor, Dr. David Wolf, said that I needed another surgery to stage the cancer. This was called a *laparotomy*, where they cut me from the base of the sternum straight down the stomach to about three inches below my belly button. They took out my spleen, a little piece of the kidney and liver, and checked the lymph nodes up and down the stomach area. I couldn't have any food or water for six full days, only ice chips and a lemon swab to keep the saliva going in my mouth. On the seventh day I got water and Jell-O.

When I got out of the hospital, I was down to 258 pounds and looked like hell. I went out to Giants stadium to watch the team practice because I think I mentally needed to be around the team. I'm not so sure that the team should have seen me. I had not only lost the weight, but because of the two surgeries, I had to carry around a pillow that I pressed to my stomach when I had to cough. It hurt like hell to cough, but I had to keep my lungs clear after having one collapsed and then having another major surgery. I felt like I turned green every time I felt a cough coming on.

But there was no cancer below the diaphragm, so I was staged at either 1B or 2A. This meant that I would only have to have radiation. I had to wait another week to get stronger, and then I started. I went for treatments at Sloan Kettering Hospital five days a week, almost like a job. The first twenty treatments were in the "mantle" area, meaning chest, underarms, and neck. The next three were "cone downs," just on the spot where the mass was, and then twenty more in the abdominal area as a precaution, even though they never found any cancer down there. Radiation, even if they radiate just the tip of your little finger, makes you very physically tired and run down. I tried to work out during this time when I felt up to it, but I was still recovering from the surgeries. I got sick only once when I pushed myself too hard when I was feeling tired. I learned my lesson and listened to my body after that.

When I was done with the treatments, I had to wait about a month for my blood counts to get back to normal. Then I had to finally get my shoulder operated on. When they went in, they found a lot more damage than they originally anticipated and had to do a very major surgery. When I woke up I was in an Orthoplast body cast with struts coming off to hold my arm in a bent position with my upper arm by my side and my lower arm pointing straight ahead. I had to keep my arm in this position for six weeks before I could move it. When I got out of the cast, the rehab started. The normal rehab for the surgery is twelve months, but I had less than six before camp. I started with just getting range of motion in my arm, then my shoulder. Then very light lifts. During the off-season program, I would do two hours of rehab, and then do the normal three-hour workout that the rest of the team was doing. All this time, I had to try to get my weight back up to about 285. All I did was work out, eat, and sleep.

I made it to camp, but the arm was still weak. I worked my ass off and it paid off. I was back in the starting lineup for the opening game of the year, which happened to be a Monday night game against Washington. Normally they do not show the players being introduced on television, but in this case they made an exception. When they announced my name I got a standing ovation from seventy-eight thousand Giant fans. The announcer waited for about a minute before he announced the next player. I had made it back.

In the second game of the year, one of my own players fell on the outside of my left leg, about eight inches below the knee. The side of my foot was lying flat on the turf of Giants stadium while I was standing straight up. I asked the doctor if I tore or just stretched the ligaments in the ankle. He said it didn't matter. I was out for seven weeks. I did not get my starting spot back.

Toward the end of the season I was feeling tired a lot. The Tuesday before the last game, I had a regularly scheduled doctor's appointment with Dr. Wolf. He found a lump by my collarbone, but said that it could be just from a cold.

We lost the last game, which knocked us out of the playoffs. I went back for a follow-up with Dr. Wolf the next week. He told me he wanted to take the lump out. I knew right then that the Hodgkin's had come back.

I had the lump removed the following week and it was Hodgkin's. Since the radiation didn't get it all the first time, it would mean chemotherapy the second time around. I ended up having seven months of chemo, a protocol called MOPP and ABV.

I was on a twenty-eight-day cycle. The first day I got two intravenous drugs, and then took two different drugs orally for the next seven days. I handled these intravenous drugs pretty well. On day eight I got three more intravenous drugs and continued one of the oral drugs for the next seven days. These intravenous drugs knocked me on my butt. I would go home from the treatments and sleep for about two or three hours and still feel lousy for about two or three days. I did not get any drugs during days fifteen to twenty-eight. During the third week my white blood cell counts (the white cells fight infection) would drop dramatically. I ended up in the hospital three different times because my white blood count dropped so low that the normal bacteria in my body ran wild and gave me a fever. The fourth week was my recovery week when I felt pretty good, then it would start all over again.

I lost my hair (and my moustache, which was the hardest thing). I didn't get that sick because I was in such good shape. It was by no means easy. I wouldn't wish chemo on my worst enemy. I still have some long-term problems from the chemo such as numbness in my feet, weakness in my hands, and fluid around my heart.

I tell people going through cancer that treatments are like training camp. No football player wants to go through training camp, but if you want to play in a regular season game, and hopefully the Super Bowl, then you have to find a way to fight through it. If a person who is diagnosed with cancer wants to live longer, then he or she has to find a way to fight through the treatments.

It is not only cancer treatments and training camp that you have to fight through. Every day every person is hit with adversity. It can be little things such as your car not starting, or it can be a major health problem. The biggest thing you have to do is not say, "Why me?" As soon as you say "Why me," you are admitting defeat. You are having pity on yourself. No one is going to pity you, but if people do, they are not helping you. You must do everything you can to get back up and get where you want to be.

The 4 Cs for Getting Through Adversity

I have a mnemonic that I think can help people through tough times. I call them the 4 Cs: *confront*, *challenge*, *conquer*, and *continue*.

First you must confront the problem. This is a three-step process. First you must admit that you have a problem. Many people just stick their head in the sand and pretend that there is not a problem. Psychologists call this denial. Some cancer patients do this, not going to treatments hoping that it will go away on its own. It will not. The second step is the "why me" stage. You must get past "why me" as fast as you can. Feeling sorry for yourself does no one any good. That will allow you to get to the confronting stage where you admit you have the problem and are ready to do something about it.

Second is challenge. Figure out a game plan for beating the problem. Make it as detailed as possible. Challenge yourself to beat the problem. If you can, challenge others to help you with your plan. Let them know that you need help to get past your problem. Get your assistant coaches, friends, players, or wife or girlfriend to help you if you need to. The more quickly you get past confronting and challenging, the closer you are to being on your way to success.

Conquering is the goal. Do whatever it takes to get here. After coming up with a game plan and having people assist you, make sure you do everything you can to help yourself.

The last step is to continue. After beating the problem, get on with your life and don't dwell on what happened or how it happened. Things that don't kill you make you better. Many people who are diagnosed with cancer and then beat it are afraid to go back to the doctor for their regular checkups. This is just stupid. Some other people are so worried about it coming back that it takes over their life and they can think of nothing else. Every time they feel the slightest thing wrong, they immediately think it is the cancer again. Get over it and get on with your life.

The first time I had the cancer, I knew very little about it. The first thing Dr. Wolf told me after telling me I had cancer was that it was the most treatable cancer there was, with a 90 percent cure rate. I was in what my wife Heidi called the "dumb jock" mode. My goal was just to get back to playing football again. I never said "why me" the first time, but it was more through ignorance. I asked the doctor what I had to do and he told me about the laparotomy, so I had it. Then he said to have the radiation treatments, so I had them. He was my coach and I was going to do what I had done for my whole life, listen to my coach and give it my best effort. When the treatments were done, then I had to get my shoulder done, so I did it. I went through the rehab, the regular workouts, and then training camp, but I was there on that Monday night for the first game in 1988.

The second time I was diagnosed, it was harder. I knew much more about cancer, so I knew I should be scared. I also knew they were doing great things with it. I did not deny that I had it, but I did go through a short period of saying, "Why me?" That is just normal human nature, but you must get past it as soon as you can. The first time I was sick, football was my driving force in getting through it. Like my wife said, I was in "dumb jock" mode. The second time my driving force was my family, which it should have been the first time also. I teamed up with my doctor again and asked what I had to do go get better. This time he asked me if I wanted to play football again. I said yes, if I could. Then I asked him why he asked. He said it might make a difference in what kind of treatments he would give. Some of the drugs had more long-term potential side effects that would make playing almost impossible. I told him football was no longer important to me and I didn't want to do this again. Give me your best shot now.

I go back to see Dr. Wolf every six months, even though he says I could push it out to once a year now. It makes Heidi feel better, so I do it. As long as he keeps kicking me out of his office saying I look great I will be happy.

I have been very open with my cancer, letting everyone know what I have been through and that they can also do it. One of the most gratifying things that has happened to me is that I have had people come up to me and say that their father or brother had cancer and was not going to get treatments, but after hearing my story, decided that he could do it. The one thing that I regret is always telling people that I was doing great even when I wasn't. During the many interviews I did, I always put a positive spin on, saying I was handling the treatments fine. I later came to find out that there were many people going through treatments who were not handling them well. Their friends would tell them that Karl Nelson was doing great with the treatments, why weren't they. It was just the attitude that you have to have as an athlete that you are indestructible and you cannot let others know your weaknesses or injuries. If I had it to do over, I would definitely tell about the problems.

I just wanted everyone to get past the "why me" syndrome, but everyone has to get there on their own.

Sources

Fowles, J. R., D. G. Sale, J. D. MacDougall. (2000) "Reduced strength after passive stretch of the human plantarflexors." *Journal of Applied Physiology* 89:1179.

Kokkonen, J., A. G. Nelson, and A. Cornwell. 1998. "Acute muscle stretching inhibits maximal strength performance." *Research Quarterly for Exercise and Sport* 69:411.

Knudson, D. 1999. "Stretching during warm-up: do we have enough evidence?" *Journal of Physical Education, Recreation & Dance* 70(7):24.

Knudson, D., P. Magnusson, M. McHugh. June 2000. "Current Issues in Flexibility Fitness" *President's Council on Physical Fitness and Sports Research Digest* 1–8.

Knudson, D., K. Bennet, R. Corn, D. Leick, and C. Smith, 2001. "Acute effects of stretching are not evident in the kinematics of the vertical jump." *Journal of Strength and Conditioning Research* 15:98.

O'Connor, R. January 2003. "Stretching—the truth." *Scholastic Coach and Athletic Director* 2(6):46.

Pope, R. P., R. D. Herbert, J. D. Kirwan, and B. J. Graham. 2000. "A randomized trial of preexercise stretching for prevention of lower-limb injury." *Medicine and Science in Sports and Exercise* 32:271.

Shrier, I. 1999. "Stretching before exercise does not reduce the risk of local muscle injury: a critical review of the clinical and basic science literature." *Clinical Journal of Sports Medicine* 9:221.

Shrier, I., and K. Gossal. 2000. "Individualized recommendations for healthy muscles." *The Physician and Sportsmedicine* 28(8):57.

Shrier, I. 2000. "Stretching before exercise: an evidence-based approach." *British Journal of Sports Medicine* 34:324.

Terjung R. L., P. Clarkson, E. R. Eichner, P. L. Greenhaff, P. J. Hespel, R. G. Israel, W. J. Kraemer, R. A. Meyer, L. L. Spriet, M. A. Tarnopolsky, A. J. Wagenmakers, and M. H. Williams. 2000. "American College of Sports Medicine roundtable: The physiological and health effects of oral creatine supplementation." *Medical Science Sports and Exercise* 32(3):706–17.

Williams, L. 1998. "Contextual influences and goal perspectives among female youth sport participants." *Research Quarterly for Exercise and Sport* 69(1): 47–57.

Index

Page numbers followed by *f* indicate that the referent appears in a figure/photo on that page.